American Character and Culture

Some Twentieth Century Perspectives

Edited by John A. Hague

Director of the Charles E. Merrill Program of
American Studies at Stetson University

FOREWORD

Some of the essays in this volume have been published previously in pamphlets under the auspices of the Charles E. Merrill Lecture Series in American Studies at Stetson University. Together with new essays by Robert Chauvin, Gerald Critoph, Marshall Fishwick, and John Hague, these articles furnish the reader with an overview of some of the striking new developments which have resulted from interdisciplinary studies in the past fifteen years. They also offer an impressive variety of fresh insights into the nature of American character and experience.

In the first section of the book the essays by Professors Critoph and Fishwick present new suggestions for interpreting and analyzing American history. Dr. Critoph, in the essay which concludes the first section, contrasts the rural and urban traditions in American life and raises important questions regarding these contending forces. Dr. Fishwick urgently demands a fresh diagnosis of the American dream. He insists that present conditions confront the scholar with evidence which requires new insights and new conceptual tools.

In the second section Professors Blake and Murphey show how interdisciplinary studies may be of service both to the humanistically and to the behavioristically oriented scholar. In his essay Professor Blake shows how history may be enriched by the use of what he calls some "uncommon sources." Professor Murphey offers a mathematically and behavioristically slanted approach to the study of group behavior. The tools which he employs will almost certainly become the basic ingredients of much multi-disciplinary study in the behavioral sciences. Thus the two articles, taken together, call upon the historian and the student of culture to cover the full span of the liberal arts curriculum.

Professors Stone and Potter, using a variety of materials, conclude that contemporary students can learn a good deal about American character by examining some special groups and traditions in American culture. Professor Stone finds that American writers have explored many of the problems of childhood, and that a careful analysis of their work can result in a redefinition of some of the platitudes about "the moral imagination of childhood." Professor Potter applies the classic interpretations which scholars have given to the American experience to the study of American women, and he finds that these interpretations do not work very well. His study raises some basic questions about the conclusions reached by Frederick Jackson Turner and David Riesman.

In the fourth section the essays examine two forces which have influenced most facets of American life, democracy and technology. Professor Persons examines one of the central political traditions in American society, and shows how twentieth century developments have created a dilemma of significant proportions. Professor Heald discusses the relationship between technology and American culture. He shows the need for a better understanding of what technology offers, and his essay points out some of the values which multi-disciplinary studies offer. Both essays contribute to the reappraisal of the American dream for which Marshall Fishwick pleads.

The final section contains an assessment of a changing region and a changing tradition. Professor Chauvin examines a variety of forces which are transforming the South and notes their impact on institutions and attitudes. Professor Hague takes a look at the romantic heritage of the American people and concludes that it is still very much with us. He also argues that many romantic character traits ought to be modified. Like Professor Fishwick he is worried about the context in which Americans pursue their dream. He finds, however, that there remains ground for cautious optimism on the part of those who seek to preserve and transmit the heritage of their civilization.

John A. Hague
DeLand, Florida
November, 1964

CONTENTS

PART  ONE

The Call for Reappraisal

DIAGNOSING THE AMERICAN DREAM

By MARSHALL W. FISHWICK

Marshall W. Fishwick is Adjunct Professor of American Studies at the University of Delaware; and Director of the American Studies Research Program, Wemyss Foundation. In these capacities he has been especially concerned with questions of theory and methodology. He is editing a volume called AMERICAN STUDIES IN TRANSITION, which the University of Pennsylvania Press plans to publish in October, 1964.

I

The play's the thing: it holds the mirror up to man. What, in our time and place, does it show?

Sounds, syntax, and logic jumbled beyond recognition. In Samuel Beckett's plays, men might sit on nothing identifiable, which exists in a gray space. The whole world crawls from left to right along an invisible track. One character resembles the square root of 2. Twenty eight people yearn for the day when their combined total ages will be exactly 1,000 years. The Butcher in Arnold Weinstein's *The Red Eye of Love* busies himself building a skyscraper out of used meat. Can *this* be "the land of the free, and the home of the brave"? What has happened to the American Dream?

The Theatre of the Absurd reveals not the rational world of our eighteenth century forefathers but a world that has gone mad. "Man attempts to make sense out of his senseless position," the brilliant young playwright Edward Albee says, "in a world that makes no sense. The social structures man has erected to 'illusion' himself have collapsed." Albee's attack on America in *The American Dream* is one of the telling documents of our generation. Our diagnosis may well begin here.[1]

---

[1] Published in 1961, the play was extensively reviewed and discussed. See, for example, *Catholic World*, Aug. 1961; *Christian Century*, March 1, 1961; *Horizon*, July 1961; *Nation*, Feb. 11, 1961; *New Yorker*, Feb. 4, 1961; *Saturday Review*, Feb. 11, 1961; and *Theatre Arts*, March, 1961. For a discussion of Albee's position in current drama, see Walter Kerr, *The Theater in Spite of Itself* (New York, 1963).

In the play his whole theme is understated. Instead of shouts and curses we confront the trite speech and clichés of everyday life, turned into a formula for ritual communication. Accurately and meticulously he reveals the neurosis inside our everyday assumptions. Suddenly we realize that individuality and creativity are squelched by the conformist way of life—killed (so far as the play itself is concerned) in the person of a foster-son murdered for disobedience. The old Emersonian phrases seem to mock us from the wings. Self-reliance merely leads to group revenge.

The Zoo Story, another Albee play, presents us with ironic suicide staged as imitation murder. Jerry, who seems unable to find any sense of community, suffers from "a great weariness." Neither Bohemian nor Beat, he simply cannot respond to the phony world around. In fact, he cannot even communicate with his landlady's dog. In reaching out for a more meaningful life, he is only moving towards his own death.

If American Studies as an intellectual enterprise in the 1960's is to be vital and effective, it must move beyond the time-honored clichés about American optimism and confront rampant pessimism. Students of our culture must move behind the façade of a chrome-covered culture and confront the main issues where they really exist.

The Great Debate of our time rages between Traditionalists and Existentialists. The former insist on keeping the inherited house tidy; the latter on discarding it and building anew. That we face unprecedented crises, no one denies. But what should our response be? Should we guard the fort, or abandon it for the frontier? Considering our predicament, what should our attitude and policy be? Anguished apprehension has brought us, in fear and trembling, to accept the paradoxicality or absurdity of the universe. Obsessed with the spectre of annihilation itself, we "rediscover" poets like Rilke; novelists like Melville; philosophers like Kierkegaard, whose comment on old-style system builders sums up our modern dilemma in a sentence: "Most systematizers stand in the same relation to their systems as the man who builds a great castle and lives in the adjoining barn."

Existentialism, which claims Kierkegaard as a fountainhead, has rapidly become a major force in the twentieth century. Some claim its origins are rooted in the ancient Greeks; others that it springs from François Villon, and after him Rabelais and Montaigne; still others see it as a reaction against the rationalism which dominated western thought from Descartes through Hegel. Whatever Existentialism's origins, it has spilled out of the philosophic

4

mould, into literature, drama, theology, politics, history, and mass media—not so much a system as a protest *against* systematizing. Particularly in the physical sciences, "laws" and "certainties" of the Newtonian world have been superseded. "To what appeared to be the simplest question," J. Robert Oppenheimer writes in *Science and the Common Understanding,* "we now tend to give either no answer or an answer which will at first sight sound like a strange catechism."

This "strange catechism" attempts to analyze the great emptiness of modern life; with nothingness that lies curled at the heart of being like a worm. Jean Paul Sartre holds that there are two kinds of being: *l'etre en soi* (being in itself) and *l'etre pour soi* (being for itself). The first is characterized by infinite density—a rock, for instance—the second by mutability and desire. Man—project plus facticity—is in the second category. Existence is action and involvement. Haunted by the gnawing passion to thwart meaninglessness, man gravitates towards ruts, pigeonholes, and fantasies. "Stop!" Existentialists cry. "Only when you struggle are you human. The uncommitted life isn't worth living."

The real enemy is inauthentic existence.[2] Its hallmarks are abstractions, circumlocutions, and pomposity. Meaning emerges only in the struggle between creativity and inquisition. "A creative period in art," Albert Camus wrote, "can be defined as an order of style applied to the disorder of an age." And again, in a poignant description of modern man's plight: "I have always felt that I lived on the high seas, menaced, at the heart of a royal happiness."

No matter what existentialism's cultural origins or terminology, its diagnosis has striking relevance in contemporary America. Wrapped in an ethnocentric cocoon, we find ourselves acting as if today's values were permanent fixtures. We are serious about trivialities (electric tooth brushes, sports cars, hair-dos), trivial about reality (life, encounter, death). We insist on convenient categorical pegs on which to hang every conception; despise uncertainty and disorder; and impose both certainty and order where none exists. So it is at home, in the market place, in the university. Instead of real education we offer adjustment, pressing pliant human beings into patterns, filling curricula with supermarket knowledge conveniently packaged and labeled. Pat answers masquerade

---

[2] A fine introduction to the subject is Paul Tillich's *Theology of Culture* (1959). See also Simone de Beauvoir, *The Ethics of Ambiguity* (1948); Jean Paul Sartre, *Existential Psychoanalysis* (1953); Jethro Bithell, *Modern German Literature,* 1880-1950 (1959); Hugh Kenner, *Camus* (1961); Thomas Hanna, *The Lyrical Existentialists* (1962); Walter Ong, *The Barbarian Within* (1962); and Gabriel Marcel, *The Existential Background of Human Dignity* (1963).

as truth. Some intellectuals have almost reverted to the eighteenth century's excessive adulation for reason. Fighting flux with formalism, they are reconciled to superficiality in every phase of life.

We accord ultimate meaning to the useful, but refuse to ask: useful for *what?* Increasingly we find ourselves being transformed into things—cogs in the universal system of organized production and consumption. We are lonely in crowds, trapped in organizations, entranced by status symbols, stripped of privacy in a naked society.

Hence W. H. Auden's caustic invitation:

> Come to our well run desert
> Where anguish comes by cable
> And the deadly sins can be bought in tins
> With instructions on the label.

He joins the long procession of those who warn against size, titilation, and triviality. A century ago Walt Whitman asserted that a mouse is miracle enough to stagger sextillions of infidels. Paul Elmer More had strong opinions about sterile abstractions:

> The absolute, the abstract, and the infinite—absolute unity, abstract being, and infinite actuality—are the most impertinent and pernicious words in the vocabulary of philosophy. Their devastation effect is in exact proportion to their lack of meaning, as a vacuum is the most deadly power in nature. These conceptions are the sterile eggs of reason never fecundated by sense; the scholar who brooks them may addle them and his own brain, but will hatch nothing.[3]

In more and more areas of American life the ability or even advisability of promulgating air-tight theories and infallible propositions is being questioned. Better honest doubt than dishonest certainty. Thus Robert A. Dahl comments on the contemporary concept of power:

> We are not likely to produce—certainly not for some considerable time to come—anything like a consistent, coherent 'theory . . . .' We are much more likely to produce a variety of theories of limited scope, each of which employs some definition that is useful in the context of the particular piece of research or theory but different in important respects from the definitions of other studies.[4]

This viewpoint has been expressed time and again by "Realists" in the field of political theory—Reinhold Niebuhr, Walter Lippmann, Hans Morgenthau, George Kennan, and Kenneth Thomp-

---

[3]Paul Elmer More, *Pages from an Oxford Diary* (New York, 1937), p. 28.

[4]Robert A. Dahl, "The Concept of Power," *Behavioral Science,* III (July 1957), pp. 201-15.

son. Learn to resist the great American impatience, they tell us; live with ambiguities which make quick generalizations untenable. Look behind the verbiage for *real* issues and positions. Make possibilities the function of actuality; but never consider actuality the only possibility.

In a more bizarre and less articulate way, America's rebels and beats have made the same point. Lacking the positive philosophy of their predecessors, those proto-existentialists in the Jazz Age Bohemia, they have nevertheless denounced sham and false rhetoric. Oscar Handlin acknowledges this in *The Americans: A New History of the People of the United States.* Norman Mailer, the beats, the hipsters, and the *sick* comedians knew what they were against, Dr. Handlin comments, but they were unable to say what they were for. The mass media deluged their generation with an array of images—confused, distorted, disordered. "Violence smothered the sentimental platitudes; they believed none of it or all of it, with equal coolness." Some pushed on to a *reductio ad absurdam.* "My name is John Filler and I represent the latest rage in American Freaklore, the hip-beat author who doesn't write," an account in the July 1963 *Esquire* began. "I don't write because it is the tradition of my school to stop, once enough insight is gained to graduate from student to mastery. You only put on paper what you hope somebody will buy. This school is sort of a fraternity, but none of us pledged it."

The historical revolution now under way, J. H. Hexter predicts, will not consist in the creation of ambitious general theories, but in piece-meal advances. Historian after historian will re-examine "the place and time with which he is mainly concerned, and [will seek] to contrive, for telling about what went on in that bounded time and place, a vocabulary of conceptions better suited to bring out its character."[5] On today's intellectual scene the force of an idea does not depend on its grandiosity.

Yet in the workaday world, discrepancies and gaps between practice and outmoded theory are ignored. Historians, David Potter notes, constantly work with separate items of data, so that relationships are a chief part of their work. "Yet," Potter continues, "the literature of their method and the procedures of their training

---

[5] J. H. Hexter, *Reappraisals in History* (New York): Harper Torch-books, 1961), p. vii. Professor Hexter's devastating attack on "tunnel history" and factor analysis make this one of the pivotal books in the field. The Social Science Research Council has been much concerned with these matters. See for example their bulletin 54, *Theory and Practice in Historical Study* (1946), Bulletin 64, *The Social Sciences in Historical Study* (1954), and *Generalizations in the Writing of History* (Chicago, 1963).

give so little attention to the systematic analysis of such relation-ships that a majority of those trained in history have never con-fronted the general question of the nature of causation or of motivation or of group identity." Many are not even aware that they *haven't* confronted these questions; many who train them are not aware of it either. To this observation John William Ward adds another. Historians seldom face the embarrassment of those in American Studies, confronting the demand to define their field. "Protected by tradition against such rude and unsettling questions, left free to do what their inclinations, conscious or otherwise, call them to, historians remain content to teach their courses and write their books, hardly bothered that their generic title refers not at all to their function but to the institutional fiction which gathers them under a single umbrella."[6]

Not only history, but all formal education runs the danger of divorcing itself from reality. Teachers abstract and generalize by inclination and habit. Students memorize phrases and formulae without learning how and when to apply them. What starts as erudition can quickly degenerate into irrelevance. Hamlet's old lament takes on new significance: "Words, words, words." Yet even the reign of words is coming to an end, along with man's bondage to the earth. Today science is able to do things that cannot be made fully intelligible in words, but only in formulae. Thus (as Mary McCarthy points out) we may be abolishing speech as vital communication between men; "and this implies that the life of action, the matching of great words with great deeds, is finished."[7]

Such basic doubts deserve primary consideration. The same generation that produced existentialism also produced American Studies.[8] Today the pressing task for those engaged in it seems not to be so much *defending* a position or culture as in defining it. *Despite* the numerical growth of American Studies departments and courses many academicians are still skeptical. In a world long marked by Cartesian fixed points, fluidity and relativism are threat-

[6]John William Ward, "Generalizations Upon Generalizations," in *American Quarterly,* XV, 3, (Fall, 1963), p. 465. In this article Dr. Ward includes the quotation from Dr. Potter which appears above; it is from an essay included in *Generalization in the Writing of History* (Chicago, 1963).

[7]Mary McCarthy, reviewing Hannah Arendt's *The Human Condition* in the *New Yorker,* October 18, 1958.

[8]In *American Studies in the United States* (Baton Rouge: L.S.U. Press, 1958) Robert Walker reports that the movement dates largely in the years since World War II. More recent summaries may be found in the *American Quarterly.*

ening. Colleagues who are friendly over coffee can become formidable in committees and departments. It is one thing to say, with Howard Mumford Jones, that the departmental system splits us into little groups conducting internecine wars; and quite another thing to do much about it.[9]

II

In so diffuse and decentralized an activity as American Studies, it is also hard to know just what has been, or is being, done. "What might be said in general terms?" Professor Riesman asked recently. "Has American Studies grown faster in state or private universities; in newer or in older ones; in universities or in colleges? How about denominational institutions? Since Robert Walker's book came out[10] there must have been great changes. Have you any sense of these trajectories? Is it still a matter of missionaries and their devoted disciples?" No one has attempted to give Professor Riesman a definite or authoritative answer.

Meanwhile, C. Vann Woodward's "Age of Reinterpretation" rushes on. Western imperialism is collapsing. New nations spring up. Power is polarized between two nuclear giants.[11] Questions of protocol and precedent are dwarfed by the titanic struggle for survival. A query once posited by an eighteenth century immigrant farmer named de Croevecoeur orbits, like a satellite, around the world: "What then *is* an American?" He is *homo sapiens* struggling in a broadbacked and boisterous culture featuring Paul Bunyan's strength and Yukon Ike's verve; Casey Jones' daring and Salvation Sal's devotion; John Henry's rhythm and Huck Finn's charm. He lives in a big, foolish, generous land, wide as the Mississippi or prairies nature hesitated to enclose; white as Cape Cod sand, black as West Virginia coal; flat as Salt Lake basin, too steep for Rocky Mountain goats.

The land is full of turbulent cities, with fingers of power reaching out into space; plantations, warmed by the glow of golden memories; river land, with earth richer than the treasures of Solomon. It abounds with poor boy sandwiches, atomic reactors, footlong hot dogs, Charles Addams gothic, Hopi Indians, imitation

---

[9]Howard Mumford Jones, *Education and World Tragedy* (Cambridge, Mass.: Harvard University Press, 1947). Pointing out that the departmental system is the creation of the last 70 or 80 years Professor Jones notes that it is "regarded by most professors as something absolute and inescapable."

[10]See footnote 8.

[11]C. Vann Woodward, *The Age of Reinterpretation* (Washington: Service Center for Teachers of History, 1960), Pamphlet No. 35.

castles, block slums, freedom marches, glass domes, beatniks, little magazines, big sells, wetbacks, greenbacks, comebacks. Fastened on it are fascinating names to set a poet musing—Dry Bones, Nantucket, Go-to-Hell Gulch, Lost Mule Flat, Machopongo, Bubbleup, Wounded Knee, Roanoke, Purgatory Creek, Lake June in Winter, Okaloacoochee Slough, and Boot Hill. Here is a group of vaguely united states searching for an epic.

In 1864 the transcendentalist George P. Marsh called this Republic "the first example of the struggle between civilized man and barbarous uncultivated nature."[12] Generally the culture hero is the savage, the theater a wilderness, and the drama one of slow progress against nature. But in America the full energies of advanced European civilization were "brought to bear at once on a desert continent." The whole process of civilization was enormously accelerated; the cultural opportunity and diversity multiplied beyond calculation.

The one valid tag for such a landscape is *pluralism*. With two powerful weapons—dynamism and the will to experiment—the continent was conquered. In the national motto and destiny, the *unum* was counterbalanced by *pluribus*. Whatever else American Studies is or is not, it must be inextricably bound up with the nation's dramatic growth and her emergence as a world power. In a positive sense, it is allied to contemporary movements within the scholarly community to regain concepts of meaning which served humanistic scholarship through the Renaissance, but which were sometimes lost in overspecialization later on. Negatively, it articulates a protest against rigid categories of knowledge, and the tendency to treat everything American as a mere extension of European culture. Both tendencies appear in essays by such pioneers in the field as Tremaine McDowell, Stanley Williams, Ralph Gabriel Henry Nash Smith, and Robert Spiller. In 1948 Professor Mc Dowell formulated his First Law of American Studies: it would present the complex design of American life, thus revealing the fundamental diversity of human experience within which the student should eventually find a fundamental unity.[13]

Ten years later the question of just *how* to present this complex design remained unanswered. Some who had manned the front line sounded a bit fatigued when they made their 1958 battle

---

[12]George P. Marsh, *Man and Nature; or Physical Geography as Modified by Human Action* (New York: Scribner, 1864). Quoted by Arthur A. Ekirch Jr., *Man and Nature in America* (New York: Columbia University Press, 1963), p. 71.

[13]Tremaine McDowell, *American Studies* (Minneapolis: University of Minnesota Press, 1948), p. 51.

report in *Studies in American Culture; Dominant Ideas and Images.*
No ready-made method for American Studies was in sight, concluded Professor Henry Nash Smith. "We shall have to develop
one for ourselves, and I am afraid that at present we shall have to
be content with a very modest program," he continued. "The best
thing we can do, in my opinion, is to conceive of American Studies
as a collaboration among men working from within existing academic disciplines but attempting to widen the boundaries imposed
by conventional methods of inquiry."[14]

Appearing five years later, Walter Johnson's brochure on
American Studies Abroad took a position which was, like Smith's,
basically conservative. In fact, he seemed more anxious to retrench
than to go forward in the far-flung outposts American Studies has
set up since World War II, thanks to the Fulbright program and
other international grants:

> It is hoped that the newly established American Studies
> Foundation [in Japan] will avoid overemphasis on the United
> States as an area study and instead will stimulate the more
> solid and productive growth of American subjects through
> the interested academic disciplines.[15]

Exporting American Studies is one of the most difficult, and
still most promising, aspects of the whole current picture. Wherever the enterprise smacks of cultural imperialism, it will be
challenged or rejected. Wherever it seeks to present an accurate
picture of a complex and powerful culture in transition, it will be
welcomed and appreciated. As Edward R. Murrow, former head
of the United States Information Agency, pointed out, we must
be willing to include "warts and all" in the picture we present.
Even the well developed academic disciplines (American literature,
history, and government) are not too well known abroad, and
run the risk of being labeled "propaganda." Courses bearing the
label "American Studies" will be more suspect still.

As early as 1953, Dr. Francis A. Young (Executive Secretary
of the Conference Board of Associated Research Councils) pointed
out that there were too few qualified candidates to meet the needs
of the Fulbright-Hays program; in 1962 the chairman of the British
Association of American Studies warned that visiting mediocrities
would do more harm than good, reinforcing rather than eliminat-

---

[14]Henry Nash Smith, "Can 'American Studies' Develop a Method?" in
Joseph J. Kwiat and Mary C. Turpie, eds., *Studies in American Culture;
Dominant Ideas and Images* (Minneapolis: Univ. of Minn. Press, 1960), p. 14.

[15]Walter Johnson, *American Studies Abroad, Progress and Difficulties in Selected Countries* (Washington, 1963). This is a special report from the U. S.
Advisory Commission on International Educational and Cultural Affairs.

ing prejudices against the United States, its universities, and its American Studies curricula.[16] By putting our house in order at home—developing mature and able scholars of American culture—we shall automatically improve our offerings overseas.

III

Meanwhile, the struggle between generalists (who would examine the macrocosm) and specialists (obsessed with the intricacy of the microcosm) continues. The former are impatient to achieve the grand synthesis. The latter insist that we must know much more about the elements we are trying to synthesize. Instead of deploring this disagreement, we should encourage it. Whether or not they concede it, each group is dependent on the other for growth and survival. The fate of interdisciplinary scholarship depends on an increase, not a diminution of questions—provided they are relevant to the issues of our time.

Let me mention six recent books which do precisely that. Despite certain weaknesses and flaws (which reviewers quickly pounced on), they point towards new ways of dealing with complex problems — perhaps even towards a new methodology for American Studies. As yet the shore is only dimly seen: but the voyage is under way.

The first title is Thomas C. Cochran's *Railroad Leaders, 1845-1890: The Business Mind in Action* (1953). Professor Cochran's primary aim is "to establish some norms of thought and attitude for American railroad presidents" between 1845 and 1890; to arrive at a "profile of presidential attitudes" on such matters as competition, social problems, expansion, and innovation. By analyzing the letter-files of 61 railroad presidents, he arrives at a picture far different from that of most historians, economists, and political scientists. He has given new insight into a complex and pivotal nineteenth century institution—the railroad.

In *The American Adam: Innocence, Tragedy, and Tradition in the Nineteenth Century* (1953), R. W. B. Lewis sets out to discover a masked pattern in American literature, and by implication in American culture. On the surface our literature shows the authentic American as a "figure of heroic innocence and vast potentialities, poised at the start of a new history." Underneath, Dr. Lewis asserts, is a very different American. The images and metaphors used in literature express masked anxieties and value

---

[16]"The Fulbright Program," *News Report* (National Academy of Sciences-National Research Council), March-April 1953, p. 22; and Johnson, *op. cit.,* p. 57.

premises. Ae we know these, a much more accurate picture of the nineteenth century American emerges.

Daniel J. Boorstin's *The Americans: The Colonial Experience* (1958) shows how American history can be reinterpreted in the light of recent interdepartmental surveys. Dr. Boorstin does not hold with the time-honored notion that America was a "second chance" for Europe; that our culture is merely an extension of the old world's. Like Turner, Parrington and Beard before him (who may be the real Founding Fathers of American Studies) Boorstin finds new categories: an American frame of mind, the ideal of the undifferentiated man, culture without a capital, the fusion of law and politics, poetry without poets, backwoods farming, and a nation of minute men. A later Boorstin book called *The Image: What Happened to the American Dream?* (1961) is more provocative, but less successful. *The Image* must be counted a failure, but a significant one.

David M. Potter's *People of Plenty* (1954) attempts to discover how economic abundance has affected American life. Can one establish a valid concept of national character by pooling the work of historians and behavioral scientists, Potter asks in his introduction; his book provides an affirmative answer. He conceives of abundance not in terms of a storehouse of fixed assets, but as something residing in a series of physical potentialities, which have never been inventoried at the same value for any two cultures. He goes on to show how some aspects of child rearing in the United States are as distinctively American (when compared with other countries) as any Yankee traits that have ever been attributed to the American people; and he opens the door to a whole series of investigations of contemporary life.

One of the most impressive recent books—*America and the World Revolution* (1962)—has the virtues of an outsider looking in. The English author, Arnold Toynbee, sees us in a perspective which natives could never hope to attain. In this study he shows how the historian can bring personal observation, moral concern, and comparative criteria into a single focus. For generations, Toynbee maintains, America symbolized the revolutionary concern of the many in a world controlled by the few. Knowing that the disease of liberty is highly contagious, Americans deliberately spread it throughout the world. By a twist of fate, we now find ourselves leading the anti-revolutionary forces. We have abandoned the world majority and joined the world minority. In our time, technology is within sight of being able to produce enough material benefits to provide for the whole human race. The millions who stand on the starvation line know this and intend to do something about it. What will the American response be?

More optimistic, and no less original, is *A New History of the People of the United States* (1963), by Oscar Handlin. His story centers on vast and lasting nervousness before a vast and lasting empty space. Handlin's theme is inner conflict and loneliness; American history echoes the ancient Greek sin of *hubris*. The rage to tame the wilderness outside and inside us has long been an obsession. We have sought security, at different times, in land, slaves, stocks, or SAC airplanes. Who are we, anyway? Does anybody know? In asking, we continue to chase Melville's white whale. That mythic beast symbolizes our uncertainty: corruption and innocence, purpose without point, invasion without destination.

Whether or not one agrees with the analysis and conclusions of Cochran, Lewis, Boorstin, Potter, Toynbee, and Handlin, he realizes that each is attempting diligently to diagnose the American dream. Instead of repeating the old platitudes, they are making fresh starts, running new tests. They seek to probe, not to pontificate.

Those who profess and practice American Studies might do well to study and emulate them. We must be equipped to perceive our uniquely American heritage, and prepared to supersede it. In a fast-changing world, the need for the kind of Americans Emerson envisioned a century ago remains: "Men and women of original perception and original action, who can open their eyes wider than to a nationality—to the considerations of benefit to the human race . . . men of elastic, men of moral mind, who can live in the moment and talk and take a step forward."

THE CONTENDING AMERICAS

By GERALD E. CRITOPH

Gerald E. Critoph is an Associate Professor of American Studies at Stetson University, DeLand, Florida. He received his doctorate in the American Civilization Program at the University of Pennsylvania and taught at Colgate and Michigan State before coming to Stetson. He teaches an introductory course in American Civilization which stresses agrarian and urban influences. His graduate courses deal primarily with American Culture in the Twentieth Century.

What is America? This is a question that has intrigued the world since the last decade of the 15th century. To many people it has meant a fabulous source of wealth. Others have seen in it opportunities not possible in countries still burdened with centuries of traditions. It has been a haven for the religiously oppressed, a second chance for social and economic failures, or an arena for making one's reputation. Because of the variety of visions which it has generated, America has attracted a broad diversity of persons to its shores. These different groups have contended for the fruits of the land and for the means of control over the land ever since. These competitive efforts have had a share in shaping the structure and the spirit of the United States as we know it today.

While the religious vision is persistent in American traditions, economic opportunity provided a greater appeal for emigrating Europeans in the 17th, 18th, 19th, and early 20th centuries. Land was the lure. To Europeans, the possession of land meant economic independence and more desirable social status. Coming from areas with limited amounts of land to a continent where it was relatively free gave the migrants hope for new life for themselves and their children.

Of course, it was not just a matter of crossing the ocean and taking up a piece of unused land. Rival forces were making claims for different distribution and use of the land. The monarchs of Europe had divided up the hemisphere and incorporated their respective portions into their empires. Imperial policy-makers usually assumed that the colonies existed for the benefit of the empire, not

15

necessarily for the colonists. This was especially true in the mercantilist era when the colonists were expected to supply the imperial masters with gold, raw materials, and markets for the developing imperial economies.

So from the beginning of its settlement, there has been contention over the meaning of America. Was it to be a conglomeration of individuals each going his own way, each following his own dream; or was it to be a well-ordered society of generally cooperative groups whose immediate goals fitted in with a universally-desired national destiny? The tensions set up in the beginning have continued to influence the development of American society: the tensions between freedom and order, between independent and collective goals, between individualism and statism.

I

Part of the motivation for autonomy and eventually independence from the British Empire came out of the feeling of frustration over individual goals blocked by imperial demands for colonial responsibility. The frontiersman, the farmer, the merchant, the embryonic industrialist, and the ambitious politician objected to the restraints (light as they were) that were imposed in the name of the British imperial system. Some Americans felt strongly enough to carry the colonies into a revolution, which the British prosecuted with great reluctance and surprising forbearance. Even in fighting for their independence the Americans resisted the temptation to organize their efforts with much unity. Only a small minority agreed with Alexander Hamilton and George Washington that national loyalty should transcend local allegiance.

The advocates of extreme individualism and localism were in the ascendancy during and immediately after the Revolution. Once the imperialists were run out of the country, there seemed no need for a strong, unified structure. The farmers went back to their land, and, since they constituted about ninety per cent of the population, there was no great impetus to establish more than the minimum of governments.

Like many another war, the Revolution was followed by an economic decline. This depression brought out a split in American attitudes. There were Americans who were beginning to play the role that British money-lenders had played before the Revolution. They were the creditors of those whose ambitions were slightly greater than their pocketbooks. On the other side ranged those who borrowed money primarily because it was a factor in produc-

16

ing goods and services, rather than something to manipulate. The split centered on disagreement as to the nature of property and the nature of man.

This division developed out of differences between two of the most influential men of the early republic, Thomas Jefferson and Alexander Hamilton. The rivalry between their visions has been so profound that it has persisted in one form or another until the present. Henry Bamford Parkes in his *The American Experience* (New York: Vintage, 1959), identifies Jefferson's view of an ideal society in terms of agrarian democracy and Hamilton's in terms of aristocratic capitalism. According to Parkes, 19th century America was able to combine the two by selecting the democracy of Jefferson and the capitalism of Hamilton, only because free land existed to absorb the inconsistencies of the conflict. The struggle has not been so patly resolved in the 20th century.

The agrarians took their cue from John Locke's assertion that each person had a right to property and that no one should have any more than he could work. The agrarians also agreed that the person who works the land should have a primary right to the land. This would include a prior right to the fruits of the land.

The Hamiltonian view emphasized the deed or grant of the land. The deed was a contract and whoever held the deed had primary right to the land and its fruits. This meant that the mortgagee and the landlord had a claim on the goods produced by the mortgagor and the tenant. Because the contract was the key to the Hamiltonian position, one of the major provisions of the Constitution assured protection of contracts and a number of Marshall's decisions reinforced their sacred nature. According to the contractual point of view, it was irrelevant who worked the land or who actually made a product. Legal possession of the land, the raw materials, and the tools of production determined who was to decide on the division of the profits.

II

Another way to look at the contention between agrarian democrats and aristocratic capitalists is in terms of the evaluation of goods and services. What were they? Were they the products of work and creative ingenuity as the agrarians claimed, or were they primarily the objects of the market to buy and sell in the process of making a profit as the capitalists claimed? The agrarians identified the goods and services with the workman; they were his, because his work had produced them. The capitalists maintained that the forces of supply and demand on the market determined the values of goods and services. This would imply that goods and services were interchangeable, therefore it was fruitless and irrelevant to identify any specific good or service with a workman. By further implication, the workman was interchangeable, so his price (or wage) was determined by forces of supply and demand on an impersonal market.

The agrarian way of life generally supported the view that each man's production was his. His goods and services drew value from his identity with them. The urban way of life tended to put market values on goods and services—what profit could be made from the transaction. As long as the farmers maintained a high degree of self-sufficiency, they could act with the independence and forthrightness that have been marked traits of the traditional American character. As the farmers increasingly produced for the urban market, they lost more and more control of their personal destinies.

III

Because the majority of Americans gained their livelihood from the soil during the first three hundred years of American history, agrarian principles formed the foundation of American traditions. By the beginning of the 19th century, these principles had been incorporated into the Declaration of Independence, a number of state constitutions, the Bill of Rights, and the writing of Thomas Jefferson and John Taylor. Their widespread acceptance was indicated by the capture and control of the government by the Jeffersonian Republicans and their successors, the Jacksonian Democrats.

The agrarian preoccupation with land was something migrating Europeans brought with them to America. Most of them aspired to the European aristocratic prerogatives that went with the ownership and control of land. They saw the possession of land as a major means to independence and self-sufficiency. Because land was so much easier to obtain in America than in Europe, it was possible for almost every family to have its own farm. This led to the family-oriented farm instead of the village or manor-oriented operation. In time, the family farm became a basic principle of the American way of life.

The ideal was a self-contained, self-sufficient farm identified with a man and his family. In the agrarian view of life, each man had to contend with the forces of nature for his success in life, not with his fellow men. His relations with other men should be occasionally cooperative, but seldom competitive. He should be self-reliant and independent of others, not only of their help but of their hindrance.

Americans could practice in large numbers the ideal of the free individual, the man who made himself what he was. They did not have to live out predetermined lives as they would have had to do in Europe. They thought of themselves as new men and of America as a new world. As R.W.B. Lewis has pointed out, in his *The American Adam,* Americans in the 19th century developed the concept of the American Adam. Nineteenth century American writers often referred to humanity's "second chance" in America and to Americans as born free of the sins of the "Old World."

Because each person is born basically good and because working with the soil in God's clean air keeps a person good, the agrarians maintained that each man could govern himself, especially if he were a farmer. If this is so, then "the best Government is that which governs least" and which is concentrated at the local levels. As a matter of fact, some American agrarians talked as though they preferred a political society close to anarchy.

In the few circumstances when agrarians considered collective action necessary, they tended to turn to what they termed "natural aristocrats." These were men who had demonstrated the wise and fruitful use of their land. Ideally, they would be those who held only the land they could work profitably and who worked profitably all the land they held.

A major agrarian precept, therefore, was that government should be in the hands of those who owned and worked the soil. They were the good men, the wise men, and the responsible men of society. In order to keep society clear of corruption, all men should have the opportunity to own and work the land. Crowding into cities should be discouraged, because the agrarians looked upon the cities and those who dwelt therein with suspicion.

As a matter of fact, most agrarians maintained that the city was a major source of evil in society. Those who had traveled in Europe in the 18th century, had, like Jefferson and Franklin, developed a fear that the growth of cities in the United States would produce bestial masses similar to those they saw in London and Paris. As cities grew in the United States, their fears seemed to be justified when large sections of the northern cities degenerated into slums.

However, slums were not the only indication of the city's evil for the agrarians. Whenever a countryman went to a city for business or pleasure, he seemed to see around him all the sins against which the Bible warns. Gambling, covetousness, stealing, murder, lying, and fornication were concentrated in such greater degrees than he saw them in the rural areas that he was convinced that the city was their origin.

As if it were not bad enough that the agrarian saw the urbanites wallowing in sin and corruption, he discovered that when he or his children went to the city they often were personally affected by the city's evil forces. Because of his innocence or naiveté, the countryman often was lured into circumstances in which his money was taken from him, or he was beaten or killed, or his pristine virtue was lost in one of the city's dens of iniquity. In the case of the country girl, American fiction and songs are full of the "fate worse than death" waiting in the city for the unsuspecting and trusting virgin.

The city slicker was a character in American agrarian mythology from the beginning of the country's history. His main goal in life was to take in the country "rube" in any way available. He cheated the countryman of his butter and egg money on market days, or he took away his farm in the form of a foreclosed mortgage and then rented the farm to the former owner at an outrageous price. The city slicker has been anything from a fly-by-night confidence man to the most powerful eastern banker or merchant. In more recent times, the industrial monopolist has taken his place among the city slickers in agrarian lore.

As a result of these images of the city, agrarians have tried to regulate commerce and banking, especially as they relate to the agricultural sector of American society. They also believed with Jefferson that industry should be restricted to a bare minimum. When this proved to be impossible in the early 19th century, they tried every way they could to keep industrial development within narrow bounds, because they saw industry as one of the most powerful forces encouraging city growth.

Industry was especially insidious to the agrarians, because they predicted, quite correctly, that industrial workers could never be completely independent of their employers. And when the industrialists began bringing shiploads of immigrants across the Atlantic and setting up company-controlled towns and cities, they were convinced that industrial workers, native or foreign, were the slaves of the employers, except in the technical sense. Therefore, the agrarians fought to keep political control of the local, state, and national governments as long as they could. The present fight against reapportionment of legislative districts is a consequence of this belief.

Some of the major American democratic beliefs resulted from the experiences of the majority of Americans in agrarian settings during the formative years of the republic. For instance, the strong, abiding conviction that a free individual's identity should be held sacred and that his dignity and integrity should not be violated was a belief that came out of situations in which an individual had to confront the forces of nature just about on his own. Life and death, success and failure appeared to be determined by personal merit.

IV

Because the agrarians were in the majority in the republic's formative years, their beliefs and their view of man and society became the dominant ones in American traditions. However, there was a growing body of urban attitudes which evolved along with, and often competed with, the agrarian. In the 20th century, some elements of these two traditions are in conflict and underlie the social, economic, and political problems of our times.

The towns and cities of 17th and 18th century America were basically commercial in origin, as were many of those established in the 19th century. They grew from settlements around good harbors on the coast, at the junctions of river branches, or where highway trails crossed rivers or other trails. In the 19th century, railroads accelerated the growth of commercial cities and brought about the rise of some new ones. As the Industrial Revolution reached the United States in the 19th century, city development took on different traits, but trade route locations still acted as a determining factor.

For the urbanite, therefore, trade has been the fundamental activity of life and the market the central mechanism of society. It would follow, then, that society's leaders were the merchants and bankers. If exchange was basic, the masters of exchange must be the fittest of all in the competitive struggle that permeated the urban scene.

Competition not only determined the social structure for the urbanites, it provided explanations for the nature of man and society. Its rules were impersonal and absolute. Their violation, for whatever reason, invited disaster. Attempts at regulating trade by any non-merchant agency has prompted strong resistance by those whose interests lie in trade.

According to the capitalist writers in 19th and 20th century United States, competition in the market operates best when each participant knows his own best interests and acts with them as ultimate goals. The argument has been that the greatest advances for society come out of the struggle among the selfish interests of society's members. So, ideally, the market mechanism with its rivalry of selfish interests should govern society, but practice demonstrated that some government was necessary to act as referee, to provide protection for property from the disgruntled losers in the conflict, and to assure a relatively stable monetary system within which to operate.

It was recognized that any government would be subject to these same principles of competing selfish interests. Therefore, the best kind of government in a capitalist society would be one in which each selfish interest was balanced by other selfish interests. Any man or small group of men could not be expected to be altruistic enough to govern others, so a constitutional system incorporating checks and balances to limit the power of any one group seemed to be the logical solution. From the beginning of the republic, one of the major arenas of contention has been in the government. Each interest group competed to gain as much control of the political machinery as it could. In this way it has hoped to get preferential treatment from the referee. One of the results of this process has been the steady increase in the size of government on all levels, despite the pious statements by almost all leaders that they were working for the reduction of governmental centralization and power.

Adherence to the unregulated, competitive, open market carries with it some contradictions. Success in the market usually leads to the increase in the size of operation. Because loyalty and cooperation within an enterprise contributes to its success, the larger an operation gets the more cooperation and collective action it demands and the less competitive impulse on an individual basis is encouraged. In addition, the organization asks that its personnel give up personal individuality to the organization. The organization men are expected to blend their identity with that of their company. The individualism touted as an essential part of the market mechanism is discouraged to ensure the success of the overall enterprise.

There are other collective tendencies connected with the demands of urban life. Industrial and commercial operations have brought together larger and larger numbers of persons to live in close proximity. Many of the necessary services for human life must be shared, instead of being obtained by personal effort. Such things as water, maintenance of health, and sewage, as well as fire and police protection seem to be handled best by some sort of collective action. In each of them, cooperation is essential to effective results.

Bringing together large numbers of persons in an area provides greater potential for educational and recreational activities. With more persons involved, a greater variety of alternatives can be offered. The more concentrated wealth of the urban communities holds possibilities for public and private educational facilities that the rural areas cannot hope to equal. Nor can the agrarians duplicate the accomplishments of the cities in the realms of music, theatre, or other entertainment which requires sums of money and reasonably large audiences to support them continuously.

The urban contradictions often result in a rhetoric that espouses the idea of the free individual in competition with other free individuals in an open market, while acting to eliminate competition and establish exclusive control over particular sectors of the community. Some of the rhetoric has been borrowed from the agrarian tradition, particularly from the works of Jefferson. This has created the appearance of a resolution of the contention between the two Americas, with the blessing of a man who has become one of America's patron saints.

V

My intention in describing the two major traditions in American life has not been to imply that they are clear-cut in definition or that the American people have been split neatly along agrarian-urban lines. As a matter of fact, because Americans are as practical and pragmatic as they are, they tend to adapt the principles and arguments that seem to provide their specific cases with plausible rationalizations. A brief summary of some highlights in the agrarian-urban conflict should illustrate some of the twists and turns it has taken.

In the early years of the republic the rival forces tended to align themselves behind Jefferson and Hamilton. The Jeffersonian Republicans contended that agriculture was man's most exalted pursuit and that land was the most legitimate form of wealth. They maintained that the leadership of society should be in the hands of the most efficient and successful tillers of the soil and that the right to select the leaders should be restricted to those whose initiative and abilities were sufficient to earn them some property. They argued that the economy and the government should favor those whose lives were related to the soil. They feared the development of commerce and industry beyond the point of providing minimum services to the agricultural sectors of society. Above all, they wished to restrict the growth of cities and towns to ensure an independent, responsible citizenry.

On the other hand, the Hamiltonian Federalists considered the general mass of Americans incapable of governing themselves. The rich and well-born were the Federalist choices for leaders and they would keep the voting franchise restricted to those owning a large amount of property. They disagreed with the Jeffersonian tenet that "the best Government is that which governs least." As a matter of fact, they advocated strong central government. This last carried the explicit assumption that the government should do all it could to encourage and advance commerce and industry.

In the first twelve years of the republic's history, Federalist control of the government established a reverence for contracts reinforced by over three decades of John Marshall's leadership in the Supreme Court. Respect for the Presidency and the central government's fiscal responsibility were other legacies from the Federalists. In somewhat ironic fashion, these erstwhile nationalists became states' rights advocates and secessionists during the War of 1812.

The Jeffersonian Republicans opposed the centralizing tendencies of the Federalist administrations, issuing the Kentucky and Virginia Resolutions advocating states' rights. However, after 1801 they found it difficult to govern without contributing to the increase in the central government's powers. Louisiana was purchased to provide room for agrarian expansion, but it was accomplished with Hamiltonian methods. The Embargo and Non-intercourse Acts were passed to maintain the nation's neutrality, but the reduction of overseas trade encouraged the industrial development that agrarians dreaded. The western agrarians were largely responsible for inciting the fervor that took the country into the War of 1812, but the capitalists gained from industrial growth and the country's leaders became convinced that a second Bank of the United States was needed for monetary self-sufficiency. They even went so far as to pass a protective tariff in 1816 that was designed to stimulate commerce and industry throughout the country.

By 1824, the agrarians in the Republican Party were beginning to feel the old suspicions toward the merchants and industrialists of the cities, especially the cities of the East. The Bank of the United States, located in Philadelphia, was gaining more power and influence to what seemed to be the detriment of the agrarians. Under the leadership of Andrew Jackson, agrarians gained control of the central government in 1829. Many had old scores to settle dating from the panics that had wiped out savings and taken away hard-earned, but mortgaged, farms.

Nicholas Biddle, president of the Bank, was confident that such a powerful institution could control the inroads of the Jackson administration. He moved against Jackson through his cohorts in Congress, Daniel Webster and Henry Clay, who were beginning to represent the moneyed and privileged interests. Jackson destroyed the Bank, but the conflict precipitated the Panic of 1837 which wiped out thousands of farmers and accelerated the Westward Movement. In the fight against the privileged groups, the agrarian defenders strengthened the central government as the agency most able to cope with great concentrations of wealth and power.

Another showdown between the agrarians and the capitalists helped to bring on the Civil War of 1861-5. By this time, however, the agrarians were split in goals and methods. The Northern and Western agrarians still adhered to the ideal of the family farm, run by an independent, self-reliant family unit. The Southern agrarians had developed what might be called an industrialized agriculture based on slave labor organized in the plantation system. In addition to these fundamental differences in style of living, the Western and Southern agrarians were further separated by the development of east-west railroad lines that linked the growing industries of the Northeast with the food and raw material-producing areas of the West.

The war replaced the plantation system with the share-crop system, which might be described as the Southern version of the family-farm model. The demands of the war accelerated the use of machinery on Western farms and contributed to the increasing dependence of Western agriculture on Eastern markets. One of the major results of the war was to establish the financial, commercial, and industrial interests of the East and Old Northwest as the directors of American destinies for the rest of the 19th century.

One of the conflicts that demonstrated this ascendancy was the struggle between the agrarians, represented by the Granges, and the capitalists, represented by the railroads. The Granger Laws, passed by a number of Western states in the 1870's to regulate the railroads, were examples of the Jeffersonian concept of local and state action by voluntary organizations of independent citizens. These laws were declared invalid by the U.S. Supreme Court on the grounds that the states did not have jurisdiction in the area of interstate commerce, according to the U.S. Constitution. The use of this Hamiltonian legacy by the railroads forced the agrarians, in self-defense, to move into the national arena where they gained the passage of the Interstate Commerce Act of 1887. While this act did not accomplish all their desired goals, it taught the agrarians that they needed to have a strong hand in national affairs.

One of the decisive battles in the war between the agrarian democrats and the aristocratic capitalists was the presidential campaign of 1896 between William Jennings Bryan and William McKinley. In one of the most clear-cut campaigns of presidential history, the Western and Southern agrarians, financed by the silver-mine owners, attempted to capture the central government from the financial, commercial, and industrial leaders of the Northeast and Midwest. A number of factors seem to have contributed to McKinley's victory: Mark Hanna's systematized collection and spending of campaign funds, effective pamphleteering against "free silver," intimidation of employees by industrialists, casting of Bryan in the role of a "dangerous radical," and the increasing aspirations of Americans for middle class comfort and respectability.

After the 1896 campaign, agrarian power and influence experienced more setbacks than successes. The United States became increasingly urbanized and industrialized, so that today less than eight per cent of the population gains its livelihood from agriculture. The farmers have been reduced to the position of just another of the interest and influence groups in our society.

Those who are successful are no longer really agrarian. While the family farm ideal continually crops up in legislation and farm literature, U. S. agriculture is becoming more and more industrialized and the farm family is acquiring more and more urban ways. In order to remain on the farm and to earn a living income, farmers have had to face the fact that their operations must be efficient, businesslike, and profitable. This has required larger outlays for machinery and more elaborate organizations. The contemporary farmer either learns to be a businessman, or he is forced to work for someone else.

As this brief sketch would indicate, the agrarians and the capitalists have not practiced either the Jeffersonian or the Hamiltonian ideals with much systematic consistency. The farmers have turned to the central government more and more to salvage what they could of their way of life in an increasingly industrial society. In addition, the small, self-sufficient unit is no longer typical in U.S. agriculture. On the other hand, while the capitalists have welcomed the subsidies Hamilton advocated (whenever they could get them), they have argued for freedom from government regulation in obviously Jeffersonian terms. At the same time, American corporate entities have become so large that they rival the government in many areas of life. It would seem that whatever explanations farmers or businessmen thought were rational, they used as legitimate arguments for their cases, regardless of whether any particular principle fitted into a logical system.

VI

Nevertheless, one of the marked characteristics of U.S. history has been the struggle between the agrarian and the capitalist conceptions of life and society. Because of the forces of economic growth, the capitalist concept of life is dominant in practice. According to the 1960 census, about 70 per cent of all Americans live in urban or suburban areas. Most work for large, complex organizations. Few own the means with which their goods and services are produced. Few can act as independent, or autonomous, self-reliant beings. What individualism is possible must be practiced within contexts somewhat narrowly defined by the organizations to which one is affiliated. For most practical purposes, the individual destinies of Americans are determined, or at least largely directed, by those whom Hamiltonians advocated as leaders—the rich and well-born.

Of course, American mythology does not readily admit this. The individual proprietorship in business and agriculture is still extolled as the ideal, even though this economic form comprises a smaller ratio of U.S. enterprise every year. Government regulation is resisted by giant corporations in the name of the small businessman. Union activity is opposed by companies in the name of the individual workman under the guise of "right-to-work" laws. Commonly-accepted individual rights are denied the members of some minority groups under the fiction that insisting on them would violate the personal right of choice held by members of the dominant groups. The interpretations of individualism have become so ambiguous and varied that American society is working out a new definition of what an autonomous individual in the second half of the 20th century can be.

While it is quite apparent that agrarianism is no longer a major force in American life, many of its principles are held to be desirable even in a highly industrialized, urbanized society. They may not be valid in the form that Jefferson expressed them, but their adaptations have wide appeal. Their validity for today's United States seems to depend on their flexibility within an increasingly corporate society and the success with which they can be used in grappling with every-day problems.

One notion that seems to maintain some of its strength is that the city is evil and corrupt. Political statements still ring with that implication. Advertisements seldom picture the joys of city life. Mass media news accounts play up the sensational and sensual aspects of it. Because more and more Americans are living in the urban areas, concerted efforts ought to be made by public and private institutions to improve urban living and to demonstrate that there are possibilities for a fruitful life in the city.

Another ideal that has clung to the American mind is the desire to own land and other forms of property. Home owners are still considered to be the more stable members of a community. They usually have more voting rights on local matters. While the independence that went with the ownership of one's own farm was not the same as the freedom of action possible in one's own home, the feeling that there is at least one place in a person's life where he can be his own boss is an attractive one for millions of Americans. The wish to own productive property has been satisfied to some extent by the ownership of corporate stock. Even though this carries with it little or no voice in company decisions, the feeling of personal independence can be increased as the size of one's stock portfolio expands.

A third agrarian principle that has been translated into urban and industrial terms is the belief that the prior right to property should go to the person who has established a squatter's claim and has put time and effort into improving that claim. This can be seen today in the labor union insistence upon seniority rights in questions of raises, promotions, and lay-offs. It has its political counterpart in legislative committee appointments and advancements.

One of the major tenets of agrarianism has lost its exclusiveness, although it maintains a great deal of appeal. That is the idea that land is *the* major source of wealth. Today, it is generally accepted that land is *one* of the major sources of wealth, sharing its place with a number of other economic factors of production.

Jefferson's vision of the United States as an agrarian republic did not come to pass. Many of the dire consequences that he foresaw for an industrial, urban United States did. They came about as byproducts of the embracing by Americans of Hamilton's vision of a well-balanced economy and a systematic cooperation between the governing and the economic forces.

As a result, the United States tends to combine an ideological rhetoric taken largely from Jefferson and his disciples with practices advocated by Hamilton and his followers. The ideology does not always square with the practice, but it provides the individual with a spirit and a set of long-range goals which carry distinctive American characteristics. These are commonly agreed to be: freedom of choice in most circumstances, equality of opportunity, and the recognition and maintenance of the rights of others.

By adhering to the Jeffersonian ideals which center on the integrity and dignity of the individual, Americans have had a tremendous opportunity to modify the crassness and materialism that lie at the base of Hamiltonian capitalism. These ideals modify the selfishness implicit in the principles of free enterprise with the tolerance and respect for others implicit in agrarian doctrines. As long as corporate, organizational life is qualified by the principles respecting the individual, Americans can claim the Jeffersonian heritage.

Generally, American historians agree that the greatness of the United States stems partly from the combination of Hamiltonian and Jeffersonian precepts. Without the cooperation and support of the government, the industrial and financial development of the country would have gone much slower and might not have gone far at all. Without the insistence upon the rights of all persons, some kind of autocratic society might have developed. Through the contending of the capitalist and agrarian impulses in U.S. society an outstanding civilization has developed with possibilities of attaining goals beyond present imagination. The problem of the present generation of Americans is to maintain the viability of their ideology in the midst of a dynamic, complex world.

PART  TWO

New Techniques: Humanistic and Behavioristic Approaches to Interdisciplinary Study

HOW TO LEARN HISTORY FROM SINCLAIR LEWIS AND OTHER UNCOMMON SOURCES

By Nelson Manfred Blake

Nelson M. Blake is Professor of History at Syracuse University. His major field of interest is American social and cultural history. His most recent publications have been THE ROAD TO RENO: A HISTORY OF DIVORCE IN THE UNITED STATES and A HISTORY OF AMERICAN LIFE AND THOUGHT.

The popularity of American studies programs gives evidence of the desire of today's students to escape the strait jackets of the traditional disciplines. By combining the study of history, literature, and the arts young people are grasping the opportunity to share in the American experience in all its variety and color. To those of us trained as specialists in some traditional field of study such programs present a challenge to rethink our conclusions and to draw insights from other types of material than those we customarily use. In this spirit, let us consider what we may hope to learn of history from literature and the arts, first in a general way, and then with specific reference to Sinclair Lewis's angry novel *Elmer Gantry*.

I

Let me explain at the outset that it is not my purpose to give much attention to the type of literature known as the historical novel. Most fiction of this type is, in my judgment, neither good history nor good literature. Even more than most fiction, historical novels are likely to be written by formula. Take one part of warm-blooded heroine and one part of devil-may-care hero, add a generous portion of violence and drop after drop of tantalizing sex, and you may concoct a synthetic marvel that will be distributed by the Literary Guild and immortalized in Technicolor Vitavision.

No doubt, this indictment is too sweeping. Some historical fiction deserves the highest praise as providing a vivid and memorable reconstruction of the past. Tolstoi's *War and Peace,* rated by some critics as the greatest of all novels, is, of course, a work of historical fiction. No American novel of comparable sweep and power has yet been written, but in the hands of men like Kenneth Roberts and Walter Edmonds our historical fiction has sometimes achieved a high level of competence. The most famous of American historical novels, Margaret Mitchell's *Gone with the Wind,* is a work of very uneven quality, but parts of it are very good indeed. Miss Mitchell's description of the burning of Atlanta is so vivid and memorable that academic historians may well read it with envy.

Even at its best, however, the historical novel is a secondary account of the past. It is true only insofar as the author has painstakingly accumulated his materials. The real historian is always impatient with learning history at second hand. He prefers to find out about the past from what he calls primary sources — that is, from the evidence left by the actual witnesses and participants of past events. It is from this point of view that literature and the arts open up the most exciting avenues for exploration.

II

Whether consciously or unconsciously, the author of a novel or a poem usually leaves a record of his own experience and observation. The nuggets to be mined out of this material are particularly valuable to the student of social history. He is interested not so much in the deeds of statesmen and generals as in what humbler people were doing and thinking. Listen to this:

Bearing the bandages, water and sponge,
Straight and swift to my wounded I go,
Where they lie on the ground after the battle brought in,
Where their priceless blood reddens the grass the ground,
Or to the rows of the hospital tent, or under the roof'd hospital:
To the long rows of cots up and down each side I return,
To each and all one after another I draw near — not one do I miss,
An attendant follows, holding a tray, he carries a refuse pail,
Soon to be fill'd with clotted rags and blood, emptied and fill'd again.[1]

These lines were written by Walt Whitman, who spent many hours comforting the wounded of the Civil War in army hospitals. Here is an authentic fragment from the past, a sensitive man writing out of his own deeply-felt experience, conveying to us a century later some conception of the grim aftermath of battle.

To the student of history, Mark Twain gives particular delight

---

[1] Walt Whitman, "The Wound-Dresser," *Leaves of Grass,* Inclusive Edition, edited by Emory Holloway (Garden City, N.Y.: Doubleday & Company, 1954), p. 260.

when he writes about mid-nineteenth century life along the Mississippi — a region he knew as an inquisitive boy and as a steamboat pilot. When Huckleberry Finn floats down the river on his raft, we get a succession of fascinating vignettes of the social history of the day. We read, for example, of Colonel Grangerford who "owned a lot of farms and over a hundred niggers." "Sometimes," says Huck, "a stack of people would come there, horseback, from ten or fifteen miles around, and stay five or six days, and have such junketings round about and on the river, and dances and picnics in the woods daytimes, and balls at the house nights. These people was mostly kinfolks of the family. The men brought their guns with them. It was a handsome lot of quality, I tell you."[2] To me, the Grangerfords in *Huckleberry Finn* are convincing in a way that the O'Haras in *Gone With the Wind* are not — and precisely for the reason that Mark Twain had seen Southern planters with his own eyes, while Miss Mitchell saw them only through the eyes of romantic imagination.

Huckleberry Finn with similar success transfers us back to the world of rural camp meetings, strolling actors, and steamboats pounding up the Mississippi at night "big and scary, with a long row of wide-open furnace doors shining like red-hot teeth."[3]

Oftentimes the sensitive description of the novelist or the short-story writer can help us to understand a whole great historical episode. Speaking of the Populist movement of the early 1890's, William Dean Howells wrote: "If anyone is still at a loss to account for that uprising of the farmers in the West which is the translation of the Peasant's War into modern and republican terms, let him read *Main-Travelled Roads*."[4] If the student of history follows this lead and dips into Hamlin Garland's famous collection of short stories, he finds such grim pictures of agricultural poverty as this:

> It was humble enough — a small white story-and-a-half structure, with a wing set in the midst of a few locust trees; a small drab-colored barn with a sagging ridge pole; a barnyard full of mud, in which a few cows were standing, fighting the flies and waiting to be milked. An old man was pumping water at the well; the pigs were squealing from a pen near by; a child was crying . . . . he could hear a woman's fretful voice and the impatient jerk and jar of kitchen things, indicative of

[2] Mark Twain, *The Adventures of Huckleberry Finn* (New York: Harper & Brothers, 1899), p. 148.

[3] *Ibid.*, p. 133.

[4] W. D. Howells, "Introduction," in Hamlin Garland, *Main-Travelled Roads* (New York: Harper & Brothers, 1899), p. 4.

ill-temper or worry. The longer he stood absorbing this farm-scene, with all its sordidness, dullness, triviality, and its endless drudgeries, the lower his heart sank. . . .[5]

Hamlin Garland's grim picture was painted in 1887. During the next decade there were remarkable changes, and Willa Cather's *O Pioneers!* depicts Nebraska of the late 1890's in quite different terms. The hardships and bitterness of frontier poverty are now mostly unpleasant memories. This is a period when hardworking Norwegian and Bohemian farmers are enjoying a modest prosperity. In Miss Cather's words:

> The Divide is now thickly populated. The rich soil yields heavy harvests; the dry, bracing climate and the smoothness of the land makes labor easy for men and beasts. There are few scenes more gratifying than a spring ploughing in that country, where the furrows of a single field often lie a mile in length, and the brown earth, with such a strong, clean smell, and such a power of growth and fertility in it, yields itself eagerly to the plough, rolls away from the shear, not even dimming the brightness of the metal, with a soft, deep sigh of happiness. The wheat-cutting sometimes goes on all night as well as all day, and in good seasons there are scarcely men and horses enough to do the harvesting. The grain is so heavy that it bends toward the blade and cuts like velvet.[6]

Social change in the cities can be similarly traced. William Dean Howells has left meticulously authentic descriptions of Boston and New York during the 1870's and 1880's. Theodore Dreiser has done the same for New York, Chicago, and Philadelphia during the 1890's and early 1900's. And James Farrell carries us on to the Chicago slums of the 1920's and 1930's. A half century of urban experience can thus be relived through the pages of these three novelists.

Obviously the realistic school of fiction is of particular interest to the social historian, but this does not mean that he can learn nothing from writers of a different tradition. If one wants to learn about Philadelphia during the yellow fever epidemic of 1793, let him read *Arthur Mervyn,* one of the Gothic novels of Charles Brockden Brown. The story itself is one of lurid melodrama, but there can be no doubt that the novelist knew from his own experience the city and the episode that served as setting for his improbable story. For a more recent period there is abundant information in the novels of William Faulkner. Faulkner is obviously no realist.

---

[5]Garland, "Up the Cooly," *Main-Travelled Roads,* p. 78.

[6]Willa Sibert Cather, *O Pioneers!* (Boston: Houghton Mifflin Co., 1913), p. 76.

Even the most biased Northerner will refuse to believe that Mississippi is exclusively populated by murderers, sadists, prostitutes, perverts, lunatics, and idiots. Yet Faulkner's horror stories are played out in a setting of great interest to the social historian. In his famous county live many authentic Southern people—small town bankers, merchants, lawyers, laborers, and household servants. The tension between the Old South and the New so often symbolized in the key figures of the novels is reflected more literally in the less grotesque minor characters—gentle folks cherishing the old traditions, aggressive newcomers, and village idlers. It is obvious that even when a novelist is writing a highly romantic or richly symbolic work he leaves abundant clues regarding the material of his own experience.

III

Literature is not the only survival from the past. Every building, every painting, every piece of music created in an earlier age and still in existence has something to tell us about the period of its birth.

If you wish to understand the Virginia society in which George Washington and Thomas Jefferson lived, visit Mount Vernon and Monticello. Reflect on the sites so carefully chosen, the formal gardens and lawns so lovingly cultivated, the large drawing rooms and dining rooms so reflective of a generous hospitality, the libraries so indicative of the bookish interests of these Virginia gentlemen. Examine what is left of the slave quarters and be reminded that a southern plantation was in fact a village, complete with its blacksmith shop, carpenter shop, spinning room, and bakery.

It is fascinating to compare this simple, dignified architecture with the ostentatious palaces of Newport, Rhode Island, built for the Vanderbilts and other millionaires during the 1880's and 1890's. Here are iron gates so ornate that it took fifty workmen a year to build them, staircases as wide as those of a railroad station, and dining rooms large enough to seat two hundred guests. To visit these Newport mansions is to see with our own eyes what Thorstein Veblen meant by conspicuous consumption.

We learn history from architecture mostly by reflection and interpretation. But painting often gives its information with unmistakable directness. For material on the seamy side of London life in the eighteenth century, what better data can there be than the engravings of William Hogarth? America has its own rich tradition of *genre* painting. George Caleb Bingham, who lived in Missouri during the 1830's and 1840's, shows us just how the fur traders, the slouching drunkards, and the top-hatted politicians of a frontier society looked. Bingham's contemporary, William Sidney Mount, lived on Long Island and depicted with equal faithfulness the daily life of his rustic neighbors. Mount is particularly valuable for his record of popular amusements like barn dancing, fiddle playing, and eel spearing. In a later day when America had become urbanized the painters derisively known as the Ash Can School painted scenes of New York City life around 1910. The work of John Sloan, George Bellows, and their contemporaries is an invaluable record of the barrooms, the skating rinks, the ferry boats, and the crowded streets of the shabby metropolis of fifty years ago.

Music is also a survival from the past. Many concert programs reflect this. We often hear a first group of compositions by Bach, Mozart or other eighteenth century composers. A second group may include works by Beethoven, Brahms, Chopin, or other nineteenth century figures. The third group may include twentieth century composers like Aaron Copland or Roy Harris. Such a program carries us through successive chapters not only of musical history but of intellectual history as well. Eighteenth century music with its restraint, its clarity, its fine sense of balance and form belongs to the world of Newton, Voltaire, and Pope. Nineteenth century music with its passion and warmth, its surging emotionalism, and its soaring climaxes belongs as clearly to the world of romanticism of Goethe and Keats and Whitman. Twentieth century music with its dissonant chords, its restless nervousness, its looseness of form reflects the intellectual trends of our own times. This is the world where the old certainties have been dislodged by the discoveries of men like Einstein and Freud. In literature the new spirit finds its outlet in experimental writers like O'Neill and Faulkner.

Sometimes the social historian can take his data even more directly from music. Nothing is more social than dancing, and the popular dance music provides data that needs no explanation. The minuet, the waltz, the polka, the foxtrot, and the Bossa Nova in their tempos and forms all speak for themselves. Genuine folk music as distinct from the synthetic variety now monopolizing the juke boxes is full of the colorful life of the past.

IV

But one may ask, are there not great dangers in drawing the materials for social history from literature and the arts? Isn't it true that writers and painters deliberately distort their materials? Everyone knows that Mark Twain was a cheerful liar indulging in outrageous Western exaggeration and that Walt Whitman had not always had the experiences that he said he had. Painters from Hogarth's day to our own have deliberately chosen their subjects to make the points that they wanted to make.

All this merely means that one must apply to these unorthodox materials of history the same standards of historical criticism that he would apply to other sources.

In the first place, one must learn as much as he can about the author or artist and why he created this particular work. This is much more important to the student of history than to the student of literature or art. To the latter the work is to a large extent an isolated object of criticism. The artist's intention is to be inferred from his creation. Its value is a matter of internal qualities of arrangement, language, symbolism, and the like. To concentrate on the artist and his background is to deal with things largely irrelevant to the making of judgments about the significance of his work.

But to the historian every author or artist is a man testifying about something that has happened in the past. We can judge the value of his testimony only if we have some kind of knowledge about the man himself. Theodore Dreiser, born of lower class German-American parentage, poorly educated, living in the cities as a struggling journalist, will look at the successful American businessman from one perspective, and Edith Wharton, born to a wealthy, old established family, carefully educated, moving with perfect ease through New York society, will deal with the businessman from quite a different point of view. Even more relevant are the philosophical assumptions underlying the work of the authors. Dreiser, eagerly swallowing all the determinist assumptions of nineteenth century science, will seize upon evidence of man's helplessness to deal with relentless social forces. Mrs. Wharton, holding a code of values in which conduct is either honorable or dishonorable, will as naturally select the evidence that supports her theory. The question always is, did a particular author or artist set out to prove anything by this particular work?

A second rule is that we must try to determine when an author or artist is working out of his own direct observation and experience and when he is using material gathered from other sources. And in the latter case we must ask how reliable these sources may have been.

Take, for example, the passage in John Dos Passos's novel *The Big Money* where he deals with events in Boston immediately preceding the execution of Sacco and Vanzetti. He describes how liberals and radicals from all over the country converged on the city, how they organized petitions and demonstrations, how they financed their activities, how the police handled them, how the Communists sought the ultimate in propaganda even if their doings might harm rather than help the effort to save the condemned men. From the standpoint of the literary critic the only question is how this episode fits into the work as a whole and whether in style and tone it contributes to the impact of the novel. But the historian must ask quite different questions. How did Dos Passos know about these events? Has he dealt with them with careful accuracy, or has he rearranged episodes to suit his literary purpose? The answers to these questions are reassuring. Dos Passos did not have to rely on old newspaper files. He himself was in Boston during these hectic days. He stood on the street near the prison at the very hour of execution. He wrote his account out of his own experience, and he told the story as it actually happened.

In using any document as historical evidence, there is still a third step to take. We must consider the probable truth or accuracy of particular statements. It is not enough to evaluate the document as a whole, as to its authorship and general characteristics. In the end, we must weigh the value of any particular item of evidence.

As a specific example, consider a paragraph from Upton Sinclair's *The Jungle,* in which the novelist is describing the processing of ham:

> Jonas had told them how the meat that was taken out of pickle would often be found sour, and how they would rub it up with soda to take away the smell, and sell it to be eaten on free-lunch counters; also of all the miracles of chemistry which they performed, giving to any sort of meat, fresh or salted, whole or chopped, any color and any flavor and any odor they chose. In the pickling of hams they had an ingenious apparatus, by which they saved time and increased the capacity of the plant—a machine consisting of a hollow needle attached to a pump; by plunging this needle into the meat and working with his foot, a man could fill a ham with pickle in a few seconds. And yet, in spite of this, there would be hams found spoiled, some of them with an odor so bad that a man could hardly bear to be in the room with them. To pump into these

the packers had a second and much stronger pickle which destroyed the odor—a process known to the workers as "giving them thirty percent."[7]

Disregarding any general evaluation of Sinclair's novel, how are we to regard these particular statements? Did Chicago packers around 1905 in sober truth doctor their hams in this way? We must recognize that Sinclair did not write out of pure imagination. He spent many weeks in Chicago gathering the material for his novel, and our knowledge of this tends to make us believe him. Yet if we are to be truly critical, we must ask a further question. Did Upton Sinclair have any bias that might affect his truthfulness at this point? And the answer to this question is disturbing. We must remember that Sinclair was not only a muckraker with all the muckraker's disposition to believe the worst about contemporary business and politics, but a dedicated socialist as well. Now I don't believe that socialists are any more untruthful than Republicans—or than college professors. But I do believe that we all have areas of passionate conviction that are likely to color our statements when we deal with certain sensitive issues. In Upton Sinclair's case, he obviously hoped to make the point that the private profit system exploited the worker and ignored the health of the consumer. The matter of the doctored hams lies so close to the central bias of the author that I think we should regard these statements with extreme caution.

The result of critically weighing these statements in *The Jungle* has not been altogether satisfactory. From one point of view, we have tended to give them credence; from another point of view, we have found reason to doubt them. Yet this is exactly the situation in which the historian frequently finds himself. When he does, he seeks further evidence. If we want to make a final judgment as to whether the Chicago packers did market spoiled hams, we shall have to study the testimony of as many other witnesses as possible.

V

Having considered both the possibilities and the pitfalls of using literary and artistic productions as sources of history, let us try out our theories in some detail with a specific document. From the literary critic's point of view *Elmer Gantry* is a bad novel—awkwardly constructed, intemperate in tone, grotesque in characterization. But the novel's deficiencies as a work of art do not necessarily destroy its interest as a document of social history. By depicting

---

[7]Upton Sinclair, *The Jungle* (New York: Viking Press, 1950), p. 134.

the condition of American church life in the early twentieth century, Sinclair Lewis provides data that may be of some value in correcting the impressions to be gathered from more pious sources.

But if we are to use the novel thus, we must first have a close acquaintance with the author. What manner of man was Sinclair Lewis? He describes his own boyhood in Sauk Centre, Minnesota, as perfectly normal—"dull school routine, skating, sliding, skiing, swimming, duck hunting."[8] Yet we may ask whether this was the boyhood he really had or the one he liked to imagine for himself. As Mark Schorer in his fine biography tells the story, Lewis's boyhood was far from happy. Lewis was always peculiar in appearance. His flaming red hair was matched with a flaming red face; he was thin and awkward; and he was the frequent butt of schoolboy jokes. At the age of seventeen this badly adjusted youth was sent away to school. First he spent six months at Oberlin Academy in Oberlin, Ohio. Though brief, this experience was important for reasons to be discussed later. The next four years were spent at Yale, where most of his fellow students detested him and he made relatively few friends.

Between graduation from Yale in 1907 and sudden fame in 1920 lay thirteen years of obscurity. After a little vagabonding adventure he supported himself by literary hack work on newspapers and in publisher's offices while he attempted to write stories and novels. Between 1914 and 1919 he published four novels, but none of them was very successful. Then came *Main Street* and a decade of great acclaim, culminating in the receipt of the Nobel Prize in 1930. After that it was mostly downhill until his death in 1951.

These are the bare facts of Sinclair Lewis's life, but they don't really tell us much about the man himself. Lewis's own estimate is that "there was never in private life a less attractive or admirable fellow,"[9] and this harsh judgment has all too much truth. Throughout life he shocked people by his extraordinary homeliness. Even when he was sober he was rude and quarrelsome, and when he was drunk—as he far too often was—he was intolerable. He was a bad husband to two wives; he was a neglectful father to two sons; he had numerous cheap affairs with women. Yet, despite all these unlovely traits, Lewis could be a highly entertaining companion.

---

[8]Mark Schorer, *Sinclair Lewis: An American Life* (New York: McGraw-Hill Book Co., 1961), p. 3.

[9]Sinclair Lewis, *The Man from Main Street: Selected Essays and Other Writings: 1904-1950,* edited by Harry E. Maule and Melville H. Cane (New York: Pocket Books, 1963), p. 47.

He was master of one thing, he said of himself, and that was of talk. A gifted mimic, he would convulse his friends by imitating "an American Babbitt boasting about his motor car, a Swede or a Yankee speaking German, a college professor lecturing ponderously on nothing in particular." If the performance sometimes seemed childish, particularly when too frequently repeated, the reason in Lewis's explanation was that he was "only practicing, only making a sketch for the next character he was to paint."[10] Pretending that he was George Babbitt or Elmer Gantry, he would improvise the long harangues that later appeared in these novels.

Explaining himself still further, Lewis said: "Besides a certain amount of lasting affection for his friends and this pyrotechnical conversation, the man seems to me to have no virtues whatever save a real, fiery, almost reckless hatred of hypocrisy—of what the Americans call 'bunk' . . . and this may not be a virtue at all, but only an envy-inspired way of annoying people by ignoring their many excellent qualities and picking out the few vices into which they have been betrayed by custom and economic necessity."[11] This "hatred of hypocrisy" is probably our most useful key to understanding Lewis's testimony about the social history of his time.

On what sources did Lewis depend when he wrote his novels? First of all, he drew on his own personal experience. Again and again bits of material are worked in that reflect Lewis's boyhood in a prairie village or his later life in other places. Of the six months that he spent at Oberlin Academy Lewis says: They were very valuable; they "gave him a notion of such small, highly pious and denominational Midwestern colleges as appear in several of his novels; and a notion of the Eastern Middlewest, in which is situated Zenith."[12] And Zenith, we must remember, is the city where not only George Babbitt and Sam Dodsworth lived but where Elmer Gantry eventually preached.

But Lewis depended not alone on his own experience but on the experience of other people. Commenting on his extensive foreign travels, he said: "The fact is that my foreign traveling has been a quite uninspiring recreation, a flight from reality. My real traveling has been sitting in Pullman smoking cars, in a Minnesota village, on a Vermont farm, in a hotel in Kansas City or Savannah, listening to the normal daily drone of what are to me the most fascinating and exotic people in the world—the Average

---

[10]*Idem.*

[11]*Ibid.*, p. 48.

[12]Schorer, *Sinclair Lewis,* p. 48.

Citizens of the United States, with their friendliness to strangers and their rough teasing, their passion for material advancement, and their shy idealism and interest in all the world, and their boastful provincialism—the intricate complexities which an American novelist is privileged to portray."[13]

So much for the witness, now let us listen to his testimony. Certainly the Reverend Elmer Gantry is one of the most unpleasant characters in all literature. What are we to think of a preacher who seduces the deacon's daughter in his first church, never gets to his second church because he gets drunk, becomes the bedmate of a woman evangelist, and finally, a hypocrite to the end, rises to fame in the Methodist Church? It would be bad enough if Lewis had written in these disrespectful terms about one preacher, but the novel depicts a score of other ministers and most of them are not much better than Elmer.

Why did Sinclair Lewis make such a savage attack upon the Protestant clergy? May it not be because we often assail with the greatest passion the things that we once have loved? It is significant that Lewis passed through a phase of intense interest in religion. As a high school boy, he attended the Congregational Church and Sunday School and was a good member of Christian Endeavor. During his six months at Oberlin he participated eagerly in the activities of the Y.M.C.A. So seriously did he take all this that he decided he was going to become a missionary. He took on a Sunday School class in a nearby village, to which he used to go by railroad hand car—exactly as Elmer Gantry goes out to his first church. After continuing these religious activities for a time at Yale, Lewis gradually lost his faith, but he still retained a high degree of curiosity about American church life.

When Lewis made the decision to write a novel about American ministers, he put himself through an unusual briefing. He struck up a friendship with the Reverend William L. Stidger, a well-known Methodist clergyman of the day, and, through Stidger, Lewis was able to organize an informal discussion group that met once a week in a Kansas City hotel room. In this extraordinary company that called itself "Sinclair Lewis's Sunday School class," there were fifteen clergymen ranging the full religious spectrum from Catholic priest and Jewish rabbi to Unitarian minister and free thinker. Lewis pumped these new friends for all kinds of information about their respective churches. Often he needled them with accusations of not really believing what they preached and of being unwilling to sacrifice for their faith. One participant re-

[13]Lewis, *The Man from Main Street*, p. 55.

members that every now and then Lewis would begin to preach with all sincerity, then he would bring himself up short and would say, "I have to stop this! I *could* have been a preacher."[14] When this group met for the last time, Lewis bade them an extraordinary farewell: "Boys, I'm going up to Minnesota and write a novel about you. I'm going to give you hell, but I love every one of you." And as each minister left the room, Lewis embraced him and said, "Good-by, old man; God bless you!"[15]

Does this help us to evaluate *Elmer Gantry?* Lewis certainly fulfilled his promise to give his minister friends hell, but where is the evidence that he loved them? The most obvious clue to the mystery is to be found in Lewis's hatred of hypocrisy. Lewis could excuse the hypocrisies of the Babbitts, but the hypocrisies of the clergy infuriated him. Speaking of himself, Lewis said: "Why, this man, still so near to being an out and out Methodist or Lutheran that he would far rather chant the hymns of his boyhood evangelicism than the best drinking song in the world, is so infuriated by ministers who tell silly little jokes in the pulpit and keep from ever admitting publicly their confusing doubts that he risks all the good friends he once had among the ministers by the denunciations of *Elmer Gantry.*"[16]

The Reverend Elmer Gantry appears to be all the separate hypocrisies that Lewis had observed, rolled into one incredible bundle of hypocrisy. For this reason, the social historian need not take Elmer himself very seriously. He is so unrepresentative of the clergy as to hardly merit consideration. More plausible, however, are Lewis's vignettes of other clergymen, in which there is some mixture of good and bad. Many of these are probably drawn from life from Lewis's minister friends. For the most part, they are a pretty poor lot also, but there are at least two ministers in *Elmer Gantry* for whom Lewis shows respect and affection. One is the Reverend Andrew Pengilly, of whom he writes:

> If you had cut Andrew Pengilly to the core, you would have found him white clear through. . . . To every congregation he had served these forty years, he had been a shepherd. They had loved him, listened to him, and underpaid him. . . . Little book-learning had Andrew Pengilly in his youth, and to this day he knew nothing of Biblical criticism, of the origin of religions, of the sociology which was beginning to absorb church-leaders, but his Bible he knew, and believed, word by word,

[14]Schorer, *Sinclair Lewis,* p. 449.

[15]*Ibid.,* p. 454.

[16]Lewis, *The Man from Main Street,* p. 48.

45

and somehow he had drifted into the reading of ecstatic books of mysticism . . . .[17]

Pengilly, Lewis implies, could be free of hypocrisy, because he had never been confronted by the challenges to faith implicit in modern knowledge, but the position of another character in *Elmer Gantry* is much more difficult. The Reverend Frank Shallard has read widely in modern science; it has shaken his faith to the point where he is really an agnostic, but he stays in the ministry. So he is, from Lewis's point of view, a hypocrite. Yet Lewis is very gentle with Shallard's hypocrisy because he understands its reasons. Shallard wishes, in the first place, to avoid giving pain to his minister-father; he also wants to protect his wife and children whom he loves very deeply. And finally Shallard sees some chance of doing good. Taunted as to why he doesn't get out of the ministry before he is kicked out, Shallard replies:

> Because I'm not yet sure—Though I do think our present churches are as absurd as a belief in witchcraft, yet I believe there could be a church free of superstition, helpful to the needy, and giving people that mystic something stronger than reason, that sense of being uplifted in common worship of an unknowable power for good. Myself, I'd be lonely with nothing but bleak debating-societies. I think—at least I still think —that for many souls there is this need of worship, even of beautiful ceremonial—[18]

Although Shallard is in many ways a weak character, Lewis portrays him in one final act of supreme courage, going through with a speech certain to bring down on him the terrible vengeance of a fundamentalist mob. Shallard is thus at last set free from all hypocrisy. In writing this passage, Lewis is certainly projecting himself. He gives to Shallard the kind of courage that Lewis wishes he had himself but knows he does not.

To the social historian these various character studies are less useful than the general excursion that Lewis conducts through American Protestantism as of about 1926. He gives an excellent picture of the way in which Methodist ministers anxiously attended their annual conferences, where they awaited uneasily the Bishop's announcement of appointments. He touches upon the problems of the urban churches occasioned by shifts of population, upon the new emphasis on ritualism among certain churches, and upon the vogue of the social gospel. Most of this is excellent reporting.

---

[17]Sinclair Lewis, *Elmer Gantry* (New York: Harcourt, Brace and Co., 1927), pp. 240-1.

[18]*Ibid.*, p. 381.

Lewis was in many ways an extraordinarily perceptive observer of the religious scene in the mid-1920's. If one can keep his temper and make proper allowances for Lewis's strong biases, he can learn as much about American Protestantism by reading *Elmer Gantry* as he can about middle-class conduct by reading *Babbitt*.

What general judgment can we make about Sinclair Lewis as a witness to American life in the 1920's? Obviously he is far from being a perfect observer. He is a man of many flaws in character. He is lacking in objectivity and judiciousness. He is strongly opinionated and oftentimes malicious in what he writes. But the judge and jury in a courtroom cannot wait for perfect witnesses. They must listen to whatever testimony is offered, shrewdly noting each witness's shortcomings and prejudices and giving to his statements such credence as they deserve. In like manner the historian must deal with Sinclair Lewis, drawing such information as he can from Lewis's rich gifts for fact-gathering and mimicry, but being constantly on guard against his weakness for exaggeration and caricature.

VI

A final word on this whole matter needs to be said. Historians, I am sure, have no wish to invade the province of other disciplines. We are not suggesting standards by which we think literature or the arts should be taught or judged. To believe that the highest value to be sought in looking at the *Mona Lisa* is an understanding of how sixteenth century Italian women wore their hair or that we ought to read *Moby Dick* chiefly for the purpose of gathering facts about the whaling industry is obviously absurd. Every great work of literature and art has both a timely quality and a timeless quality. The historian is particularly interested in the data that the work reveals about the age in which it was created. The critic, on the other hand, is properly concerned with the things in the work which are as true for us as they were for the author or the artist. *Moby Dick* and *The Scarlet Letter* are great novels because they deal with problems and conflicts that beset men in every age, such problems as evil, sin, guilt, and remorse.

All that I am attempting to say is that literature and art have their secondary delights—and one of these is that they hold the mirror to the society that produced them. I am entirely certain that historians should read more novels and poems, look at more buildings and paintings, and listen to more music. I am almost as sure that students of literature and art should read more history.

CULTURE, CHARACTER, AND PERSONALITY

By MURRAY MURPHEY

Murray Murphey received his Ph.D. in American Studies at Yale University in 1954. He is currently Associate Professor of American Civilization at the University of Pennsylvania. His major book is THE DEVELOPMENT OF PEIRCE'S PHILOSOPHY.

Since Fromm published *Escape From Freedom*[1] in 1941, the study of national character, and more generally of group personality, has become exceedingly popular. Psychologists and psychoanalysts, political scientists, and even historians have contributed to the ever growing literature on the subject. As is usually the case with new fields, the rapid growth of both data and theory has been accompanied by some vagueness respecting the basic terms employed and their relations, and this has been particularly true respecting the relations between culture and personality. Some investigators have been accused of psychologising the culture: others of culturizing the personality; some have held that personality and culture must be defined so as not to overlap; some hold that the concepts necessarily overlap.[2] There is, in short, considerable confusion in the field as to what personality is and how it is related to culture.

Definitions of personality are a dime a dozen, and few of them agree. This does not mean that most of them are wrong, although they may be; it rather means that "personality is defined by the particular empirical concepts which are part of the theory of personality employed by the observer."[3] Definitions of personality therefore are theory-specific. Accordingly, to discuss the relation of personality and culture in any reasonable way, one must start from a

---

[1] Eric Fromm, *Escape From Freedom* (New York: Rhinehart and Co., 1941).

[2] See the critical reviews of the literature in Alex Inkles and Daniel Levinson, "National Character: The Study of Modal Personality and Sociocultural Systems," in *Handbook of Social Psychology,* Linzey, ed. (Cambridge: Addison-Wesley Co., 1954). II, pp. 977-1020, and H. C. J. Duijker and N. H. Frijda, *National Character and National Stereotypes* (Amsterdam: North-Holland Publishing Co., 1960).

[3] Calvin Hall and Gardner Lindzey, *Theories of Personality* (New York: John Wiley and Sons, 1957), p. 9.

theoretical basis which affords such a definition. Moreover, this theoretical basis must be sufficiently articulated with the concepts used to describe the culture so that relations between personality and culture can be discussed. For purposes of this paper I shall adopt the stimulus-response theory (hereafter the SR theory) as such a basis. Whether the same results would be obtained on the basis of Freudian theory or field theory or McClelland's theory or the many other possible choices is a question which must be left to the proponents of those approaches.

I

In their brilliant book on child training and personality, Whiting and Child[4] also took SR theory as a basis. In order to relate the concepts of SR theory to those of culture, Whiting and Child sought to define the necessary cultural concepts in terms of the concepts of SR theory.[5] The basic definition they use for this purpose is the difinition of "custom"—*viz.* "A custom is a characteristic habit of a typical member of a cultural category of persons."[6] Here the term "custom" which is a cultural concept is defined in terms of "habit" which is a term of SR theory characterizing individual behavior. The definition does indeed relate these two terms, but it also involves other terms which are not terms of SR theory— *e.g.,* the term "characteristic" as here used is distinctively a cultural concept. So far as Whiting and Child are concerned this fact creates no problem: they do not claim that custom is definable solely in SR terms and the definition as they give it does all that they require. But it is a question worth exploring whether or not custom can be defined solely by concepts of SR theory together with those of logic and mathematics. In fact, it is my contention that this can be done. Before endeavoring to justify this contention, however, we must clarify the meaning of Whiting and Child's definition.

There are three terms in the definition whose meanings are not obvious. When they speak of a "cultural category of persons," Whiting and Child mean any set of persons in a society who are distinguished by the members of that society as a distinct group.[7] By "typical" they "mean a central tendency such as the mode or the median but arrived at by the ethnologist's judgment."[8] The

---

[4]John W. M. Whiting and Irvin L. Child, *Child Training and Personality* (New Haven: Yale University Press, 1958).

[5]*Ibid.,* p. 16.

[6]*Ibid.,* p. 22.

[7]*Ibid.,* pp. 22-23.

[8]*Ibid.,* p. 23.

use of subjective rather than objective methods of determining the central tendency was due to the nature of the data: the authors would certainly have preferred objective methods had they been applicable. Finally, by "characteristic habit" they mean that "the habit must in some way be relevant to a person's membership in the cultural category."[9] The relevance here spoken of however is very complex. A simple association between membership in a category and performance of a given habit would not satisfy this definition: neither would a habit performance of which is a condition for becoming a member of the category. What Whiting and Child mean to describe is such a relation between the category and performance of the habit that the habit is performed because the person is a member of that category.

The basic concept of SR theory which is relevant to the concept of custom is habit. As Whiting and Child define it, "a habit is a relationship between a set of stimuli and a response (or series of responses) such that there is a probability that when the simulus is perceived by a given organism the response will be evoked."[10] Several points about this definition require emphasis. First, habits are general. The stimuli in the stimulus set are not identical although they are similar—the degree of similarity being measurable in j.n.d's[11] and the same holds of the response set. The habit therefore is a connection among members of one class and members of another, not between one stimulus and one response. Second, we extend the habit concept to situations in which a given stimulus evokes a series of responses $r_1 \ldots r_n$ if reinforcement follows r_n but no preceding member of the series, and all responses from r_1 to r_n are conditioned to the stimulus. Third, the probability of the response being evoked by the stimulus is a measure of the "habit potential" of the habit in question (Hull's effective reaction potential).[12]

There are several types of habits of which we shall have need, and we may conveniently adapt the definitions used by Whiting and Child for most of these. A "belief" may be defined as a habit whose response symbolizes some relationship between events.[13] A "practice" may be defined as a habit "whose response directly affects a change in the environment, the performer, or the relation-

[9]*Ibid.*, p. 24.

[10]*Ibid.*, p. 18.

[11]Just noticeable differences. Cf. Clark Hull, *Principles of Behavior* (New York: Appleton-Century-Crofts, 1943).

[12]Whiting and Child, *Child Training,* p. 18, n.1. Hull, *Principles,* pp. 283-284.

[13]Whiting and Child, *Child Training,* p. 28.

ship between the two."[14] A "positive sanction" may be defined as a habit whose stimulus is the performance of a habit (or the failure to perform a habit) in given stimulus conditions, and whose response is a reward to the individual performer (or non-performer). A "negative sanction" may be defined as a habit whose stimulus is a performance of a habit (or the failure to perform a habit) in given stimulus conditions, and whose response is a punishment to the performer (or non-performer).[15] A "value" may be defined as a habit whose response attributes goodness or badness to some event.[16] A "motive" may be defined as a habit which is responsible for acquired drive in its performer, and a "satisfaction" as a habit which is responsible for acquired reward in its performer.[17] These definitions follow Whiting and Child precisely except that these terms are here defined in terms of habit rather than custom. The reason for this is that individuals can have beliefs, values, motives, satisfactions and practices and exercise sanctions, so that these terms should first be defined for individuals and then extended to groups. It should also be remarked that the terms "reward" and "punishment" are well defined concepts of SR theory: a reward is that which reduces a drive, a punishment is that which creates pain.[18]

To these definitions we now add a further one. For any phenomenon y and any individual x, x recognizes y if and only if there exists a verbal expression V which is used by x to designate y uniquely—*i.e.* to designate y and y alone. This definition coordinates recognition with the possession of a unique linguistic designation and implies that what cannot be named cannot be recognized. This thesis concerning the relation between language and consciousness is by no means new—it was asserted by Freud and has been incorporated into SR theory by Miller and Dollard.[19] By its use we obtain a definition of recognition which, like those of belief, practice, and sanction can be stated wholly in SR terms.

For habits to be customs, they must stand in peculiarly complex relations to social groupings. Any society may be regarded as a set of n people: by a well known theorem there are then 2^n-1

[14]*Ibid.*, p. 27.

[15]*Ibid.*, pp. 29-30.

[16]*Ibid.*, p. 28.

[17]*Ibid.*, p. 30.

[18]Hull, *Principles*, p. 131. Neal Miller and John Dollard, *Social Learning and Imitation* (New Haven: Yale University Press, 1941), pp. 41-42.

[19]John Dollard and Neal Miller, *Personality and Psychotherapy* (New York: McGraw-Hill, 1950), p. 158.

non-empty subsets of this society. Any such subset might have associated with it certain characteristic behaviors, but as a rule only a few of these subsets actually do have a significant relation to behavior. Thus in our society women, priests, and lawyers do have peculiar behavioral patterns, but 35th cousins, brunettes, and men born on the third of March do not. Which subsets a given social system utilizes in its division of tasks is an empirical question of considerable interest: some subsets have distinctive behavior in all societies while others are behaviorally significant only in a few, or in none.

A subset may be recognized, or it may not. If it is, then there exists some set of people who recognize it—*i.e.* who use a distinctive linguistic expression to designate that subset. Thus "women" designates uniquely adult females, and "men who wear spats" designates uniquely a certain class of men. It should be stressed that it is the use of the expression as a name which constitutes recognition: the fact that everyone in the society uses the words "men," "wear," "who," and "spats" does not mean that they apply the expression "men-who-wear-spats" as a set name. It is also important to see that recognition of a subset does not imply that its members have distinctive behaviors: we all recognize brunettes, but there is no distinctively brunette behavior. Finally, recognition is a relation between a set recognized and a set of recognizers. In any complex society there are many subsets having characteristic behaviors which are recognized by only a small fraction of the total society. This is obviously true in our own society where there are thousands of job classifications known only to a minute fraction of the total population.

Habits may be related to sets of people in many different ways. The simplest such relation is ordinary association—a statistically significant relation between performance of a habit and membership in a given set. Such associations are obviously of great importance and much of the research done in social science is concerned with relationships of this sort. Nevertheless, this is not the sort of association between habit and set that constitutes custom. In fact, the relationship which makes a habit a custom involves at least three sets of people and four kinds of habits. In the first place, there are the performers of habit—the members of what Whiting and Child call the cultural category. Let us call the set of these people X and the members the x's. Secondly, there are those who recognize X and have beliefs about the behavior of the x's. It is not necessary that all who recognize X should have such beliefs, but it is necessary that all who have such beliefs should recognize

X. Let us call the set of believers Y and its members the y's. Third-ly, there are those who perform sanctions upon the x's. Let us call this set Z and its members the z's. What relations must obtain among these sets? Clearly, all x's are y's, for performance must be guided by beliefs about the performance. It is also clear that all z's must be y's, for sanctions are applied as behavior does or does not conform to expectations, and such expectations are beliefs. But the x's need not be z's, although they may be. The x's can per-form perfectly well without exercising sanctions upon themselves, although they cannot perform without beliefs about their perform-ance.

To say that a habit h_1 is "characteristic" of X, in the sense in which Whiting and Child use this term, comes I think to saying that the y's believe that the x's perform h_1 and that the z's sanction the x's for such performance or the failure to perform. This is not indeed an explication of the meaning of "characteristic" but rather an assertion respecting the necessary and sufficient conditions for a habit's being "characteristic" in that sense, but I think it will be generally agreed that these conditions are necessary and sufficient. It is because certain people expect that habit of the x's and because some people reward and/or punish the x's as they do or do not perform the habit that being an x is relevant to the performance of that behavior.

Whiting and Child defined a custom as a habit characteristic of a "typical member" of a cultural category of persons rather than as a habit performed by all members of the set. They explained their preference for the "typical member" approach by raising two objections to a definition in terms of shared habits. First, there are customs which characterize single member sets, as *e.g.* the Presi-dent of the United States. If "shared" is taken to mean "common to more than one," then clearly no shared habits characterize a single member set, while if "shared" is construed reflexively then every habit of the single member is a custom.[20] A possible answer to this objection is that although there is only one president at a time still there have been thirty-six presidents over a period of time, and the customs of the presidency are the habits characteriz-ing all thirty-six presidents. But this answer seems to me clearly fallacious. Had the office of president been abolished in 1796, it would still be true that there were customs characterizing the presi-dency which were not mere idiosyncracies of Washington. A better answer is provided by the definition given above, for accord-

[20]Whiting and Child, *Child Training,* pp. 23-24.

ing to this definition being shared is not a necessary condition for a habit to be a custom. It is only habits which are expected and sanctioned which are customs, and there can be expectations about and sanctions upon one person as well as many. Accordingly, Whiting and Child's objection does not touch the definition here offered.

But the objection does bring out the very significant difference between customs and habits which are merely shared by a group of people, and this is a difference which raises some important problems in itself. In the definition of custom given above, we made use of several types of shared habits—the beliefs of the y's and the sanctions of the z's. Are these shared habits customs or not? The answer must obviously be no, so far as the above definition is concerned: otherwise we should be defining custom by custom. Yet it is also obvious that those beliefs and sanctions can be customary: there might be a set W of people who recognize Z and expect z's to sanction x's and there might be a set U of people who sanctions the z's for their performance of (or failure to perform) sanctions upon the x's. The important point is that we can determine whether or not a given habit is a custom without knowing whether the beliefs and sanctions which make it a custom are customary themselves. The definition of custom is therefore not circular: it refers to shared habits but not to other customs.

A further point about this objection should also be remarked. Suppose that $X = Y = Z = [x]$: i.e. suppose X, Y, and Z have all only one member, x. Then is the habit in question a custom or not? It seems to me to make little difference which way we decide this question. Common usage does permit a man to refer to an idiosyncratic habit as his "custom," but such a usage violates somewhat the spirit of the concept as used by Whiting and Child. Accordingly, we should probably require that if X is a unit set, then X does not equal Y and Z does not equal X.

But Whiting and Child raise a second objection to the shared habit definition of custom which also applies to the definition given above. Within any reasonably large set of people there will be considerable variation in the performance of the custom. It is therefore inaccurate to speak of one habit being shared by all: we should rather speak of a limited range within which these variations fall.[21] There are two answers to this objection. First, it should be noted that habits themselves are general. A habit is a relation between a class of similar stimuli and a class of similar responses, so some variation is permitted within the concept of habit itself. Nevertheless, it is easy to find cases in which this

---

[21]*Ibid.*, p. 24.

answer will not suffice. For example, it may be customary in a society to greet strangers, and there may exist several forms of greeting which are equally acceptable but which are not similar. In this case all members of the society do greet strangers, yet there is no shared habit of greeting.

There are two cases here which must be clearly distinguished. If the form of greeting depends upon characteristics of the stranger, or of his behavior, then there is no problem: we have simply several distinct habits with different stimulus sets, but each habit is shared by the whole society. Thus, if all Irishmen salute all Germans and shake hands with all Frenchmen, there are simply two distinct customs each of which characterizes all Irishmen. The case which makes trouble is the case in which the stimuli are the same but there are different responses occurring with comparable frequency among the Irish, as *e.g.* if half shake hands and half bow, irrespective of the characteristics of the stranger or of his behavior. In this case, the shared habit definition of custom clearly collapses altogether.

But the objection also points to the way to its own solution, for as Whiting and Child note, "culture does not mean precise uniformity but merely restriction of the range of variation in behavior."[22] What we have here is a set of habits which fall within the accepted limits of variation. We may define this class of equally acceptable alternatives in the following way: it is a class of habits $h_1 \ldots h_n$ such that each member of the class has an identical stimulus set, and at least one of the two following conditions is met; either, if any x performs any one of the habits $h_1 \ldots h_n$ but not the others then the z's positively sanction x, or, if any x performs any one of $h_1 \ldots h_n$ then no z negatively sanctions x, and if some x does not perform one of $h_1 \ldots h_n$ then the z's negatively sanction that x. This amounts to a definition of a class of habits which the z's—*i.e.* the sanctioners—regard as equally acceptable. We may then define the custom of the x's as this set of habits equally acceptable to the z's. These habits need have no more in common than their stimulus sets, which makes them genuine alternatives to each other, and their acceptability, which makes them equally acceptable alternatives. Habits need not be shared to be customs, but they must be equally acceptable responses to given stimuli. If the responses which the x's habitually make to a given stimulus set are equivalent, then that equivalence class of habits is a custom, and in the limiting case where all x's make the same response, the custom is a shared habit.

---

[22]*Ibid.*, p. 24.

There is a further reason for preferring this definition to that given by Whiting and Child—namely, the lack of clarity of the concept of a "typical member." Whiting and Child define 'typical' as "a central tendency such as the mode or the median but arrived at by the ethnologist's judgment."[23] A central tendency is a characteristic of a distribution, and a distribution is a distribution of a variable. But in the phrase, "typical member of a cultural category of persons," it is not at all clear what variable is referred to. Consider for example the cultural category of women. What is the "modal woman?" If we consider the variable "height of a woman" then a modal value, and even a mean value, can be defined, since this variable has a distribution. But unless such a variable is specified, the phrase "modal woman" is meaningless. Nor is it obvious how to make the specification. For purposes of defining a habit as a custom, it would appear that the "typical member" must be typical with respect to his performance of the habit concerned. But in that case the "typical member" is defined in terms of the "typical habit," and the phrase "characteristic habit of a typical member, etc.," becomes "characteristic habit of a member having the typical habit," which is far from clear. It is true that in describing the habit characteristic of a set of people it will very often be necessary on any definition to use measures of central tendency, but these measures must be applied to characteristics of the habit, not the performer. There are many variables on which habits may vary (habit potential, latency, amplitude of response, etc.) and a typical habit will be one which represents the central tendencies of these diverse variables. But it is the habit, not the member, which is typical.

II

If the argument given above is correct, then it appears that we can give a definition of custom which contains nothing but terms of SR theory, mathematics, logic, and set theory. What are the implications of this conclusion for culture theory as a whole? It must already be apparent that there is a strong analogy between the concept of custom presented above and the concept of role. Indeed, a role will appear in this theory as a complex of customs, or more precisely, as a set of equivalent habit complexes characterizing a set of people in the same way that a custom does. The specification of the exact nature of the complex which constitutes a role is too broad a subject to be treated here: what does need

---

[23]*Ibid.*, p. 23.

urging is that the relation of role and status is the same as that between custom and the set of performers, and that roles differ from individual customs only in being equivalence classes of complexes of habits rather than equivalence classes of single habits. And if role and status are definable in these terms, then so is the social structure as a whole, for the social structure is just the system of roles and statuses characterizing the society. It seems a fair inference, therefore, that the whole of the non-material culture is reducible to these components. A proof of this thesis would require a book, but I think sufficient grounds have already been given to make it plausible, and I will therefore entertain this hypothesis for the remainder of this paper.

From the standpoint of SR theory, the personality is the structure of drives and habits characterizing the individual. This structure includes other people and their behavior as stimuli to which the individual responds, but the drives and habits and their organization lie within the individual. Culture, on the other hand, is the system of drives and habits which characterizes the group. It includes of course what is common to all members of the group, but it is particularly concerned with interrelations among the individuals and subsets of the group. Both personality and culture, therefore, are structures or organizations of drives and habits.

This assertion respecting the nature of culture and personality contradicts a number of well known views. Some writers, seeking to avoid an overlap between culture and personality, relegate behavior to culture, and restrict the personality to the organization of non-behavioral psychological states and processes which are inferred from behavior and which are conceived as causes or conditions of the behavior.[24] But such an emasculation of the concept of personality seems hardly defensible. As the term "personality" is used in ordinary language it refers to an individual's characteristic ways of responding to stimuli, and such responses may obviously be behavioral. Most theorists employ the concept of personality as an integrating concept referring to the organization of the psychologically significant components of the person. To exclude behavior from the personality is therefore to deny that it is psychologically significant—a procedure which seems dubious at best. Habits involving behavioral responses are constituents of both culture and personality and little is accomplished by denying so obvious a fact.

On the other hand, there are definitions of culture which differ

---

[24]Duijker and Frijda, *National Character,* p. 38. Ralph Linton, *The Cultural Background of Personality* (New York: Appleton-Century-Crofts, 1945), p. 84.

radically from that given above. Some writers use the term culture to refer to behavior patterns which are norms for the group, while other patterns are relegated to what is called the "social system."[25] But this usage need not be debated, since it only means that what I have called culture above, these writers call culture plus the social system. Other writers restrict culture solely to behavior and exclude all reference to drives and motives which they regard as belonging to an extracultural domain of personality. Yet such writers do regard sanctions as legitimate components of culture, and a sanction cannot be defined without reference to drives in the individual. Thus one cannot define a particular role in a given society without reference to the sanctions used to enforce conformity to the role prescriptions, and to say that a given act of z on x is a positive sanction for x is to say that it is drive reducing for x. Accordingly, these writers do include references to drives in their expositions of culture, albeit implicitly.

What is the relation of culture and personality? Both are constructed from the same elements—drives and habits. Each represents a particular organization of those elements. Personality is the organization of these elements in the individual: culture is their organization in the set of people. If we find a given habit which characterizes all members of a set, that habit is a component of the culture; but it is also a component of the personality of each person who holds it. It is true that there may be habits in some personalities which are neither shared with others nor related to the beliefs and sanctions of others, and these habits we exclude from the culture as idiosyncratic, but every habit in the culture is first in some personality.

Nevertheless, many writers insist that culture and personality are radically distinct, and even that "culturally determined" behavior is not only not personality but also not indicative of personality. At its extreme, this position leads to the absurdity of saying that deviant behavior is more expressive of personality than conformist behavior, because, forsooth, deviant behavior is not determined by the culture so it must be the result of personality![26] What seems to underlie such arguments is the fact that some habits are intrinsic to the person while others are not. Indeed, if personality is simply an organization of drives and habits, then some habits must be intrinsic—in fact, constitutive—of personality, in such a sense

---

[25]Duijker and Frijda, *National Character*, pp. 40-41. Cf. Talcott Parsons and Edward Shils, ed., *Toward A General Theory of Action* (Cambridge: Harvard University Press, 1960), Part I.

[26]Duijker and Frijda, *National Character* p. 42.

that their alteration would create a new or different personality. But other habits appear to be extrinsic in such a sense that dropping those habits would not create a new or different personality. If one then says that the extrinsic habits are performed because they are enforced "by the culture" while the intrinsic habits "spring from the personality," one is in effect saying that intrinsic habits are those enforced by sanctions which the performer applies to himself while extrinsic habits are those in which the performer does not sanction himself but others do. Hence, since deviant behavior is (allegedly) not sanctioned by others, it is not extrinsic —therefore it is intrinsic.

The argument has its merits. Habits clearly do differ in some such way as that indicated by the intrinsic-extrinsic division, but this difference is a matter of degree. The organization of drives and habits constituting the personality is complex, and clearly some habits will have a more central role in that organization than others. One may expect that habits which carry strong self-sanctions are probably more central to the structure than those which carry little self-sanction, and it is reasonable to assume that the more central to the structure a habit is, the more far-reaching will be the consequences of its alternation. On the other hand, it seems doubtful that there are many behaviors performed by a person which are wholly devoid of self-sanctions of some kind. People are rarely indifferent toward behavior which they perform frequently. Moreover, even if a particular performer does not sanction himself for performing a given habit, still performance of that habit may be a means of obtaining a self-administered reward if it is followed by positive sanctions from another, and such positive sanctions are a stimulus to self-congratulation in the performer. Thus the interrelations among the component drives and habits of the personality can be very complex and devious, and there are probably very few habits performance of which is not in some respect self-sanctioned.

It follows from these remarks that conformist behavior very likely involves self-sanctions: indeed, there is no reason why those habits most central to the personality may not be fully in accord with the expectations and sanctions of others. For most people, most of the time, customary behavior affords the most thoroughly satisfying method of drive reduction. Nor is there any reason to believe that deviant behavior is somehow a better expression of personality than conformist behavior. Deviance need not be self-sanctioned: it can arise from a host of factors, such as role contradictions, conflicting demands of different sanctioning groups, means-ends situations where an approved means to the goal is not available, etc., which have as little, and as much, to do with personality as those which operate to induce conformity.

If personality is an organization of drives and habits characteristic of the individual, then a group personality is an organization of drives and habits characterizing the members of a particular set of people. The problem of how such an organization becomes associated with this set may then be approached in the same way that we approach the problem of how any complex of habits and drives becomes associated with a particular set. The simplest case of this sort is that of custom, in which a single habit, or a set of equivalent single habits, is induced in the members of a set of people. A more complicated case is that of role, in which a complex of habits, or a set of equivalent habit complexes, is induced in the members of a set of people. Viewed from this perspective, group personality is simply a case in which a still more elaborate complex of habits is induced in the members of the set, and what makes a personality customary will be essentially the same factors which make all habit complexes customary.

We are accustomed to viewing role as a complex of habits induced and maintained in the members of a set of people by the expectations of others and the due application of sanctions to the members of the set according as they do or do not perform the expected behavior. We are accustomed to viewing personality as a complex of habits and drives instilled in the individual by a process of child rearing and thereafter enduring with only slight modification until death. Both views require revision. If we consider the training to which a candidate for a role is subjected, it is clear that a large part of this training consists in the induction of appropriate motives, values, and satisfactions and in internalizing in the candidate a set of rules the violation of or conformity to which by the candidate will result in self-sanctioning responses. Role training thus involves both the organization of drives already present and the acquisition of new ones as well as the learning of practices and beliefs—a fact which is dramatically evident in the case of the training for such roles as the priesthood. Similarly, if we consider the induction of personality in an individual, it is clear that what we call child rearing is a process in which the child is led to conform in thought, action, and feeling to the expectations of others, and the means by which this conformity is obtained is the due application of sanctions by some set of sanctioners—usually the parents—according as he does or does not conform. Moreover, it is obvious that the formation of personality does not terminate at six, or twenty-one, or even forty: personality is continuously modified, whether by life or psychotherapy, until death. The behavioral complex which is the role is thus a subsystem of the personality, and the personality, if it characterizes a set, is in a generalized sense a role. Being a doctor is the same kind of phenomenon as being an Englishman.

Personality and culture are not identical. There will be in every individual personality some elements which are purely idiosyncratic. But where an organization of drives and habits sufficiently extensive to qualify as a personality characterizes the members of a set of people, we are dealing with a cultural phenomenon. We do not hesitate to classify less extensive organizations of drive and habit such as roles as cultural phenomena: why should we hesitate to do so with personality? Of course the culture is much more than just an aggregate of personalities, since it involves various kinds of relations among them and among their constituents, but group personality is as much a part of culture as custom or role.

From this perspective, it should be clear that the problem for culture and personality studies is not the interaction of personality and culture. To ask how personality and culture interact makes about as much sense as to ask how the planets interact with the solar system. The significant problem is how drives, habits, and social groupings are related. To determine the modes of personality characteristics—*e.g.* aggressiveness—in a given society is usually fruitless unless we also determine how those characteristics are related to specific groupings and to the drives and habits of people in other sets. This has in fact been the focus in child rearing studies, which have for this reason been the most interesting of the group personality studies, and in those few splendid studies such as Hallowell's work on the Ojibwa[27] which have made the field worth while. But such studies are not numerous and a raft of major problems remains virtually untouched. The attempt to divide culture from personality has created a pseudo-problem—the interaction of culture and personality—which has led us away from the problems which ought to engage our interest—the interrelations of drives and habits in individuals and sets of individuals.

---

[27]A. Irving Hallowell, *Culture and Experience* (Philadelphia: University of Pennsylvania Press, 1955).

PART THREE

Two Special Groups: Women and Children

AMERICAN WOMEN
AND
THE AMERICAN CHARACTER

By David M. Potter

*David M. Potter is Coe Professor of American History
at Stanford University. His interest in the type of social
history represented by this article began with the publication, in 1954, of PEOPLE OF PLENTY. He is
currently engaged in a study of the historical aspects of
alienation in the United States, under a grant from the
Carnegie Corporation.*

There is an old riddle which children used to ask one another
concerning two Indians. One was a big Indian, the other was a
little Indian, and they were sitting on a fence. The little Indian,
the riddle tells us, was the big Indian's son, but the big Indian was
not the little Indian's father. How, asks the riddle, can this be?

Boys and girls for a long time have found that this riddle
succeeds very well in mystifying many people. And the fact that it
does presents another puzzle as to why the riddle is hard to answer.
If we were to state the question in more general terms: there
are two human beings, one adult and one child; the child is the
son of the adult, but the adult is not the father of the child, probably no one would have much difficulty in recognizing that the
adult is the mother. Why then do the Indians on a fence perplex
us? If we examine the structure of the riddle, I think we will find
that it contains two devices which inhibit our recognition that the
big Indian is a female. First, the two Indians are described as being
in a very specific situation—they are sitting on a fence. But women,
at least in our culture, do not usually sit on fences; if the two
Indians had been roasting some ears of corn, or mending their
teepee, how much easier the riddle would have been. Second, we
are perhaps especially prone to think of Indians as masculine. If
the riddle had said two South Sea Islanders, or perhaps, two Cir-
cassians, the possibility of their being female might occur to us
much more easily.

But most of all, the riddle owes its baffling effect to the fact
that our social generalization is mostly in masculine terms. If we

65

said that the little Indian is the big Indian's daughter, but that the big Indian is not the little Indian's mother, the possibility that the big Indian is the father would come to mind readily enough. For in our culture, men are still in a general category, while women are in a special category. When we speak of mankind, we mean men and women collectively, but when we speak of womenkind, we mean the ladies, God bless them. The word humanity is itself derived from *homo,* that is man, and the species is *Homo sapiens.* Neuter nouns or general nouns which are ambiguous as to sex— nouns like infant, baby, child, sibling, adolescent, adult, spouse, parent, citizen, person, individual, etc.,—all take masculine pronouns. In our culture, a woman, at marriage, takes her husband's name. Though born a Cabot, if she marries Joe Doaks, Mrs. Joe Doaks she becomes and Mrs. Doaks she remains, usually for the rest of her life.

This masculine orientation is to be expected, of course, in a society which is traditionally and culturally male-dominated—in what we call a patriarchal rather than a matriarchal society. Even women themselves have connived at maintaining the notion of masculine ascendancy, and in the rather numerous concrete situations in which they actually dominate their men, they often dissimulate their control by pretending to be weak, dependent, or "flighty." In such a situation one must expect that men will be regarded as the normative figures in the society, and that, in popular thought at least, the qualities of the masculine component in the society will pass for the qualities of the society as a whole.

If this habit were confined to popular thought, it would hardly be worth examining. But it also sometimes creeps into academic and scholarly thought, which ought to have more rigor, and when it does so, it can sometimes distort our picture of society. Thus a writer may sometimes make observations on the traits or values of American men, and then may generalize these as the traits or values of the American people. If he did this deliberately, on the theory that since male values dominate the society, they must therefore be American values, we would have to concede that he is aware of what he is doing, even though we might question his results. But when he does so unconsciously, his method may easily lead him to assume first that since American men are dominant, the characteristics of American men are the characteristics of the American people, and that since women are people, the characteristics of the American people are the characteristics of American women, or in short, that the characteristics of American men are the characteristics of American women.

To avoid this trap, when one meets with a social generalization it is frequently worthwhile to ask concretely, does it apply to women, or only to the masculine component in the population? Does the statement that Prussians are domineering mean that Prussian women are domineering, or only Prussian men? Does the statement that Americans are individualistic mean American women as well as American men? The question seems worth asking, for it appears more than possible that many of our social generalizations which are stated sweepingly to cover the entire society are in fact based on the masculine population, and that if we took the feminine population into account, the generalization might have to be qualified, or might even run in an entirely different direction.

I

A notable example of this can perhaps be found in Frederick Jackson Turner's famous frontier hypothesis, stated so brilliantly at Chicago almost seventy years ago. The gist of Turner's argument was, of course, that the frontier had been a basic influence in shaping the character of the American people. Primarily, as he saw it, the frontier provided economic opportunity in the form of free land. When this free land was suddenly conferred upon a people who had previously been held in dependence by the land monopolies of the Old World, it made the American economically independent and this independence made him more individualistic and more egalitarian in his attitudes. Also, the necessity for subduing the wilderness by his own personal exertions, in a situation where he could not call upon doctors, dentists, policemen, lawyers, contractors, well-drillers, repairmen, soil analysts, and other specialists to aid him, made him more self-reliant.

Not even Turner's harshest critics deny that there was much truth in his observations, but many of them have pointed to his lack of precision, and it is fair to question to what extent Turner's generalizations applied to all frontier people, or to what extent they applied restrictively to frontier men. Sometimes it becomes clear that the life-process which he identifies with the frontier was primarily though not wholly an experience shared by men rather than by women. There is one famous passage, for instance, which begins, "The wilderness masters the colonist." Now *colonist* is a neuter noun, and could apply to a female colonist. But the passage continues to say that the wilderness, finding the colonist "European in dress, industry, modes of travel, and thought, . . . takes him from the railroad car and puts him in a birch canoe [this sounds

67

progressively less as if it could be a woman.]. It strips off the garments of civilization and arrays him in the hunting shirt and the mocassin." Soon, this colonist hears the call of the wild almost as clearly as Jack London's dog, and when he does, " he shouts the war cry and takes the scalp in orthodox Indian fashion."[1] Here, at least, the pioneer in question is hardly a woman.

Certainly it is true that the frontier offered economic opportunity, and certainly, also, frontier women shared in some of the social consequences which flowed from the fact that this opportunity was available to their men. But is it not true, in cold fact, that the opportunities offered by the West were opportunities for men and not, in any direct sense, opportunities for women? The free acres of the West were valuable to those who could clear, and break, and plow and harvest them. But clearing and breaking, plowing and harvesting were men's work, in which women rarely participated. The nuggets of gold in the streambeds of California in 1849 represented opportunity to those who could prospect for them. But the life of the prospector and the sourdough was not a woman's life, and the opportunities were not women's opportunities. Similarly, the grass-covered plateau of the Great Plains represented economic opportunity for those who could use it as an open range for the holding and grazing of Longhorn cattle. But the individuals who could do this were men; the Cattle Kingdom was a man's world. Thus, when Turner says that "so long as free land exists, the opportunity for a competency exists," he means, in effect, an opportunity for males.

Again, it may bear repeating, there is no question here that the frontier influenced women as well as men. It had its Molly Pitcher and its Jemima Boone, as well as its Davy Crockett, and its Kit Carson. It left its stamp upon the pioneer women as well as the pioneer men. But when Turner states that it furnished "a new field of opportunity, a gate of escape from the bondage of the past," one must ask, exactly what was the nature of women's participation in this opportunity? Before this question can be analyzed, it is perhaps necessary to recognize that women's place in our society is invariably complicated by the fact that they have, as men do not, a dual status. Almost every woman shares the status of the men in her family—her father or her husband—and if this is a privileged position, she is a recipient of some of the privilege. This is an affiliated status, but if her men gain, she gains with them. Thus, if her family became landowners on the frontier, she participated in their advancement, and no one can deny that free land was, in this in-

[1] Frederick Jackson Turner, *The Frontier in American History* (New York: Henry Holt and Co., 1920), p. 4.

direct sense, opportunity for her also. But woman also has a personal status, which is a sex status, as a female. As a female, on the frontier, women were especially dependent upon having a man in the family, for there was no division of labor there, as there was in settled communities, and most of the tasks of the frontier—the hunting, the wood-chopping, the plowing—could hardly be performed by women, though many of them, of course, rose to these tasks in time of emergency. In fact, the frontier was brutally harsh for females, and it furnished its own verdict on its differential impact upon the sexes. "This country," said the frontier aphorism, "is all right for men and dogs, but it's hell on women and horses."

If we accept Turner's own assumption that economic opportunity is what matters, and that the frontier was significant as the context within which economic opportunity occurred, then we must observe that for American women, as individuals, opportunity began pretty much where the frontier left off. For opportunity lay in access to independent employment, and the employments of the frontier were not primarily accessible to women. But in the growing cities, opportunities for female employment began to proliferate. Where the work of the frontier called for the strong back and the powerful muscles of a primeval man, the work of the city —clerical work, secretarial work, the tending of machines—has called for the supple fingers and the ready adaptability of a young woman, and it was in this environment, for the first time in America, that women found on any scale worth mentioning, access to independent earning power. Once woman possessed access to such earning power, whether she used it or not, the historic basis for her traditional subordination had been swept away. The male monopoly upon jobs was broken, and the breaking of this monopoly was no less significant for American women than the breaking of the landlord's monopoly upon fertile soil had been for American pioneer men. As a symbol, the typewriter evokes fewer emotions than the plow, but like the plow, it played a vital part in the fulfillment of the American promise of opportunity and independence. The wilderness may have been the frontier for American men, and the cabin in the clearing the symbol of their independence, but the city was the frontier for American women and the business office was what gave them economic independence and the opportunity to follow a course of their own.

II

Another social generalization which is often stated as if it applied to all Americans, men and women alike, is that our society has experienced a vast transformation in the occupational activities of its people, and that we have passed from the independent, self-directed work, of the kind done by a land-owning farmer, to the regimented, externally-directed activity of the employee who labors for pay. In 1850, 63% of the gainfully employed workers in the United States were engaged in agriculture, and a high proportion of these were land-owning farmers—perhaps as nearly independent as people can be. In the past the farmer, more than most of his fellows, was in position to plan, decide, and act for himself—to maintain his own values without regard for the approval or disapproval of his fellow man, to work at his own pace, to set his own routine. But today, as the census figures show, the American who labors is no longer self-employed. In 1958, it was estimated that 50,000,000 people gainfully employed in the United States received salaries or wages, while only 8,000,000 were self-employed, which means that in general the American worker does not work for himself. He works under direction in an office or a factory. He does not decide what to do, when to do it, or for what purpose, but he waits for instructions which come to him through channels. Even the junior executive, despite his prestige, is no more a self-employed man than the factory worker, and if we may believe *The Organization Man* he is in fact considerably less independent after hours. With these ideas in mind, we speak in broad terms about the disappearance of the old forms of autonomous, self-directed activity.

Yet none of this applies in any sense to women, except for women who are employees, and although female employment has increased steadily to a point where nearly one-third of all women are employed it is still true that two out of three American women are not employees, but find their occupation chiefly in the maintaining of homes and the rearing of children. Millions of housewives continue to exercise personal choice and decision not only in arranging their own time-table and routine but also in deciding what food the family shall have and how it shall be prepared, what articles of purchase shall have the highest priority on the family budget, and, in short, how the home shall be operated. Despite strong tendencies toward conformity in American life, it is clear that American women exercise a very wide latitude of decision in these matters, and everyone knows that there are great variations

70

between the regimes in various American homes. Indeed it seems fairly evident that the housewife of today, with the wide range of consumer goods available for purchase and the wide variety of mechanical devices to free her from drudgery, has a far broader set of alternatives for household procedure than the farm wife of two or three generations ago.[2] Moreover there are now great numbers of women working independently in their own homes, who a generation ago would have been working very much under direction as domestic servants in the homes of other women. If we based our social generalizations upon the experience of women rather than that of men, we might drop the familiar observation about the decreasing independence of Americans in their occupational pursuits. Instead we might emphasize that in the largest single occupational group in the country—the group which cooks and rears children and keeps house—there is a far greater measure of independent and self-directed work than there was in the past.

III

Closely connected to this question of the disappearance of the independent worker is another commonplace generalization, namely that the American people have become the victims of extreme specialization. Everyone is familiar with the burden of this lament: American industry has forced the craftsman to abandon his craft, and with it the satisfaction of creative labor, and has reduced him to operating a machine or to performing a single operation on the assembly-line as if he were a machine himself. Further, the complaint continues, modern conditions provide fewer and fewer opportunities for a worker to be an all-round person of varied skills and resources, as the American farmer used to be, and instead conditions make of him a diminished person, a narrow specialist hardly fit for anything save his narrow specialty.

Despite the exaggerated and somewhat hackneyed character of this outcry, it contains an important element of truth as regards the work of American male workers. But this generalization, too, is in fact applicable largely to the male component in the population rather than to the American people as a whole. For the American housewife is not a specialist, and in fact her modern role requires that she be far more versatile than her grandmother was, despite

---

[2]Robert Lynd, "The People as Consumers," writes that there is "probably today a greater variation from house to house in the actual inventory list of family possessions . . . than at any previous era in man's history." *Recent Social Trends in the United States* (New York: McGraw-Hill, 1933), pp. 857-911.

the greater skill of the grandmother in cooking, sewing, and other household crafts. A good housewife today must not only serve food to please the family palate, but must also know about calories, vitamins, and the principles of a balanced diet. She must also be an economist, both in her knowledge of the quality of the products offered to her and in her ability to do the impossible with a budget. She must not only maintain a comfortable home, but must also possess enough skill in interior decoration to assure that her own ménage will not seem dowdy or unappealing by comparison with the latest interiors shown in Hollywood films. She must not only rear children, but must also have mastered enough child psychology to be able to spare the rod and still not spoil the child. She must not only get the children ready for school, but must also, in many cases, act as a kind of transportation manager, participating in an elaborate car pool to convey them to and fro. In addition to all this, society now enjoins her not to rely upon the marriage vows to hold her husband, but to keep her personality and her appearance so attractive that he will have no incentive to stray. Whatver else she may be, she is certainly not a specialist, and even if she fails to meet all these varied demands upon her, her mere effort to do so would remove her from the category of specialists. If we based our social generalizations upon women rather than upon men, we might quite justifiably affirm that the modern age is an age of diversified activity rather than an age of specialization.

IV

The profound difference between the patterns of men's work and women's work are seldom understood by most men, and perhaps even by most women. In terms of the time-tables of life, however, the contrasts are almost startling. For instance, man usually begins work in the early twenties, labors at precisely timed intervals for eight hours a day and five days a week, until he is sixty-five, when his life as a worker may be cut off with brutal abruptness and he is left idle. Woman also usually begins work in the early twenties, perhaps in an office on the same time-table as a man, but after a very few years she becomes a wife, whose work is keeping house, and mother whose work is rearing children. As such she labors often for from fifty-one to fifty-six hours a week, and she does not have the alternation of work and leisure which help to lend variety and pace to the life of her husband. Her work-load will continue to be heavier than her husband's until the children are older, after which it will gradually diminish, and she may ultimately re-enter employment. But most women do not; they continue to keep house.[3] And as long as a woman does keep house, either as a wife or as a widow, she never experiences the traumatic, sudden transition from daily work as the focus of life to enforced idleness—the transition which we call retirement.

Another far-reaching consequence of the difference between man's work and woman's work is forcibly expressed in a recent public interest advertisment in *Harper's Magazine* by Frank R. Neu, entitled "We May Be Sitting Ourselves to Death." Neu presents some very impressive data about the poor physical fitness of a large percentage of American men, and about the deleterious effects of the sedentary life of Mr. Joe Citizen as an officeworker whose principal exercise is to go around a golf course on an electric cart on the week-end. Then Mr. Neu says "Let's consider Jill, Joe's wife, for a moment. Chances are, on the basis of current statistics, Jill will outlive Joe by anywhere from five to 25 years. Medical science is not sure yet whether this is because Jill has different hormones from Joe or whether it is a result of the different roles which Joe and Jill fulfill in our society.

"The average suburban Jill is likely to be a home-maker re-sonible for rearing two or more children. It is safe to assume that any woman with this responsibility is going to get a lot of daily exercise no matter how many gadgets she has to help her do the housework. A homemaker does a lot of walking each day merely to push the buttons and start the machines that wash the clothes, cook the meals, and remove the dust. And she also does a good deal of bending each day to pick up after Joe and the junior members of the family. All in all, Jill is likely to get much more exercise than Joe. This may have a significant relationship to Jill's outliving Joe, who no longer hikes the dusty trail to bring home the buffalo meat and hides to feed and clothe his family."[4]

In the light of differences so great that they may radically alter the duration of life, it is again evident that a serious fallacy results when generalizations derived from the experience of American men are applied indiscriminately to the American people in such a way as to exclude the experience of American women.

---

[3]In 1957, of the 21,000,000 women in the work force, 11,000,000 were wives. Female employment was highest (45%) in the age brackets 20 to 24, declined to 39% in bracket 25 to 44, rose to 40% in the bracket 45 to 64, and declined to 10% in the bracket 65 and over.

[4]*Harper's Magazine,* Vol. 223 (Nov., 1961), p. 23.

As a further illustration of the readiness with which one can fall into a fallacy in this way, let me suggest one more generalization about Americans which has been widely popular in recent years. This is the proposition, formulated by David Riesman in *The Lonely Crowd,* that the American has been transformed, in the past century, from an inner-directed individual to an other-directed individual. A century or so ago, the argument runs, the American learned certain values from his elders, in his youth. He internalized these values, as matters of principle, so that, in Riesman's phrase, they served as a kind of gyroscope to hold him on his course, and he stood by them throughout his life whether they were popular or unpopular. When these values were involved, he did not hesitate to go against the crowd. Thus he was inner-directed. But today, says Riesman, in a universe of rapidly changing circumstances, where the good will of our associates is more important to our success than it ever was to the nineteenth century farmer, the American no longer internalizes his values in the old way. Instead, he responds very perceptively, very sensitively, to the values of others, and adjusts his course to meet their expectations. Indeed their expectations are a kind of radar-screen for his guidance. Thus he is other-directed, or to use an older and less precise term, he is much more a conformist.

Riesman does not discuss whether his thesis about "the changing American character" is applicable to American women, as well as to American men.[5] But we are entitled to ask, does he really believe that American women were so inner-directed as his analysis would suggest? Perhaps yes, if you believe that women have been more steadfast than men in defending the values on which the security of the home is based. But on the other hand, woman, historically, was a dependent person, and as a dependent person, she developed a most perceptive sensitivity to the expectations of others and a responsiveness in adapting herself to the moods and interests of others. She has always had a radar screen. If women are quicker to conform to the expectations of a group of other women than men are to a group of other men, and if we should say that this

---

[5]David Riesman, *"The Lonely Crowd:* A Reconsideration in 1960" in Seymour Martin Lipset and Leo Lowenthal, eds., *Culture and Social Character: The Work of David Riesman Reviewed* (Glencoe, Ill: The Free Press, 1961), p. 428, discusses an investigation by Michael S. Olmsted which showed that Smith College girls regarded themselves as more other-directed than men and regarded other girls as more other-directed than their group, but Riesman does not state what his own belief is in this matter.

has been true in the past, what it would mean is that women have been other-directed all along, and that when Riesman says Americans are becoming other-directed, what he means is that American men are becoming other-directed. As women gain more economic and social independence, it might be supposed in terms of Riesman's own analysis, that more than half of the American people are becoming less other-directed rather than more so. With the gradual disappearance of the so-called "clinging vine" type, who dared not call her soul her own, this is, in fact, apparently just what is happening.

VI

If many of the generalizations which apply to American men, and which purport to apply to Americans generally, do not actually apply to American women, anyone who attempts to study the American character is forced to ask: to what extent has the impact of American historical experience been the same for both sexes, and to what extent has it been dissimilar? Viewed in these terms, the answer would probably have to be a balanced one. Certainly the main values that have prevailed in American society—the belief in individualism, the belief in equality, the belief in progress, have shaped the thought of American women as well as of American men, and American women are no doubt more committed to individualism, and to equality, and to progress, than women in many other societies. But on the other hand, some of the major forces that have been at work in American history have impinged upon men and upon women in differential ways. For instance, as I have already suggested, the frontier placed a premium upon qualities of brute strength and of habituation to physical danger which women did not possess in the same degree as men, either for biological or for cultural reasons. The result has been a differential historical experience for American men and American women which must be analyzed if there is any basis to be found for asserting that there are differences in the character types of the two sexes.

What then, we might ask, have been the principal transformations that history has brought in the lives of American women? Surprisingly enough, this is largely an unexplored field, but there are certain answers which appear more or less self-evident.

One of these is that our society has, during the last century and a half, found ways to do most of its heavy work without the use of human brawn and muscle. Water-power, steam power, electric power, jet power, and the power of internal combustion have largely eliminated the need for brute strength and great physical stamina in most forms of work. This transformation has emancipated men to a revolutionary degree, but it has even more strikingly emancipated women, for women are physiologically smaller than men, and they lack the muscular strength and physical endurance of men. As the factor of hard labor in human work is reduced and the factor of skill is enhanced, therefore, women have found that inequality in ability to meet the requirements of work is greatly diminished. This basic fact, by itself, has probably done more than anything else to promote the equality of women.

But if this is the most fundamental effect of the mechanization of work, mechanization has also had a number of other sweeping consequences. One of these is that it has destroyed the subsistence farm as a unit of American life, and the disappearance of the subsistence farm, in turn, has had the most far-reaching implications.

To appreciate this, we must remember what life was like on the subsistence farm. The only division of labor that existed in this unit was the primitive division between men and women. The men constructed the dwelling, planted and cultivated the crops, raised the cattle and hogs and poultry, sheared the sheep, and chopped wood for the stoves and the fireplaces. In short the man was the producer—the producer of food, of fuel, of the raw materials for clothing. The farm wife, in turn, not only cooked, kept house, and cared for the children, as modern wives still do, but she also performed certain other tasks. She used ashes to make her own soap, she put up vast quantities of preserved food, she spun fibers into cloth, and made cloth into garments. In economic terms, she and her daughters were processors. Together, they worked in a small, close-knit community, in which all lived very much together.

It hardly needs saying what happened to this typical unit of life in an earlier America. The use of machinery, the increased specialization of labor, and the development of an economy of exchange superseded it, and rendered it almost obsolete. Today a limited number of farmers with machines raise enough food for the entire population. Men go out to work instead of working on their own place, with their own sons, and their reward is not a harvest but a weekly wage or a monthly salary. Instead of "making a living" they make an income. All this is obvious, and oft-repeated. But what are the implications for the American woman?

Some embittered critics have retorted that modern woman, no longer a processor of goods, has lost her economic function, and that she retains only a biological function as mate and mother and a social function in the family. This loss of function, they would

76

say, accounts for the frustration and sense of futility which seems to plague modern woman even more than it does modern man. But if we take a hard look at this argument, clearly it will not stand up. What has happened is that women have acquired a new role, in a new division of labor. With her husband away from the home, held by the compulsions of the clock, it falls to her, first of all, to use the family's income to take care of the family's needs. In short, while her husband has changed from a producer to an earner, she has changed from a processor to a consumer in a society where consumption is an increasingly important economic function.

The responsibilities of the consumer are no mean task. To handle them successfully, a person must be something of a dietitian, a judge of the quality of many goods, a successful planner, a skillful decorator, and a budget manager. The business of converting a monthly sum of money into a physical basis for a pleasant life involves a real art, and it might be counted as a major activity even if there were not children to rear and meals to prepare. But the increased specialization of the work of men at offices and factories away—frequently far away—from the home has also shifted certain cultural duties and certain community tasks in ever-greater measure to women.

In the Old World, upper-class men, claiming leisure as the principal advantage of their status, have made themselves the custodians of culture and the leaders in the cultural life of their communities. In America, upper-class men, primarily businessmen, working more compulsively and for longer hours than any other class, have resigned their cultural responsibilities to women and then have gone on to disparage literature and the arts because these pursuits, in the hands of females, began to seem feminine. Women have shouldered the responsibility, have borne the condescension with which their cultural activities were often treated, have provided the entire teaching force for the elementary schools, and most of the force for the secondary schools, and have done far more than their share to keep community life alive. This is another of the results, impinging in a differential way upon women, of the great social transformation of the last two centuries.

VII

So far as we have examined them, all of these changes would seem to operate somewhat to the advantage of woman, to have an emancipating effect, and to diminish her traditional subordination. No longer handicapped by a labor system in which biceps are at a premium, she has moved into the realms of employment, and has even preempted the typewriter and the teacher's desk as her own. If she has exercised a choice, which she never had before, and has decided to remain in her home, she has encountered a new economic role as a consumer rather than as a processor, with a broad range of activities, and with a new social role in keeping up the vigor of the community activities. In either case, the orbit of her activities is far wider than what used to be regarded as women's sphere, and it has been wide enough in fact to lead some optimistic observers to speak of the equality of women as if it were something which had reached some kind of absolute fulfillment and completeness about the time of the ratification of the woman's suffrage amendment in 1920.

Yet before we conclude our story with the ending that they all lived happily ever after, it is necessary to face up to the fact that women have not found all these changes quite as emancipating as they were expected to be. Indeed, much of the serious literature about American women is pessimistic in tone, and makes the dissatisfactions and the sexual frustration of modern American women its principal theme. Great stress is laid upon the fundamental dilemma that sexual fulfillment seems to depend upon one set of psychological attitudes—attitudes of submissiveness and passivity—while the fulfillment of equality seems to depend upon an opposite set—attitudes of competitiveness and self-assertion. At its grimmest level, this literature stresses the contention of Sigmund Freud that women instinctively envy the maleness of a man and reject their own sex. There is no doubt that these psychoanalytic views are important and that attention to questions of the sex life of an individual is basic, but a very respectable argument can be and has been made that what women envy about men is not their maleness in purely sexual terms but their dominance in the society and their immunity from the dilemmas which the needs of sexual and biological fulfillment on one hand and of personal fulfillment on the other pose for women.[6] The inescapable fact that males can have

---

[6]Probably the best of the literature which emphasizes the sex frustration of the modern American woman is found in professional publications in the fields of psychology and psychoanalysis which do not reach a popular audience. In the literature for the layman, probably the best presentation of this point of view is Simone de Beauvoir's excellent *The Second Sex* (New York: A. A. Knopf, 1953), but other items have enjoyed a circulation which they hardly deserve. Two cases in point are Ferdinand Lundberg and Marynia F. Farnham, *Modern Woman: The Lost Sex* (New York: Harper, 1947) and Eric John Dingwall, *The American Woman: an Historical Study* (New York: Rinehart and Co., 1958). Denis W. Brogan's judicious and yet precise evaluation that Dingwall's book is "strictly for the birds" would be equally applicable to Lundberg. For

offspring without either bearing them or rearing them means that the values of family life and of personal achievement can be complementary for men, where they are conflicting values for women.

This one immutable and timeless fact, more than anything else, seems to stand forever in the way of the complete and absolute equality of men and women. Political and legal emancipation and even the complete equality of women in social relations and in occupational opportunities could not remove this handicap. So long as it remains, therefore, no one who finds a measure of inequality still remaining will have to look for an explanation in social terms. But it is legitimate to ask whether this is the only remaining barrier to emancipation, or whether other factors also serve to maintain adverse differentials against woman, even in modern America, where she seems to be more nearly equal than she has been in any other time or place, except perhaps in certain matriarchal tribes.

There are, perhaps, two aspects of woman's role as housekeeper and as consumer which also contribute, in a new way historically, to work against the prevailing tendencies toward a fuller equality. These aspects have, in a subtle way, caused society to devalue the modern activities of women as compared with those of men, and thus may even have contributed to bring about a new sort of subordination.

One of these is the advent of the money economy, in which income is the index of achievement, and the housewife is the only worker who does not get paid. On the farm home, in the days of the subsistence economy, neither she nor her husband got paid, at least not very much, and they were economic partners in the enterprise of making a living. But today, the lowliest and most trivial job which pays a wage counts as employment, while the most demanding and vital tasks which lack the sanction of pecuniary remuneration do not so count. A recent, and in fact very able book entitled *Women Who Work* deals, just as you would expect, not with women who work, but with women who get paid for their work. Sociologists regard it as an axiom that the amount of income is as important as any other criterion in measuring social status today, and in one sense, a woman's status may reflect the income of her husband, but in another sense it should be a corollary of the axiom that if income is esteemed, lack of income is followed by lack of esteem, and even by lack of self-esteem. If it needed

an able argument that the condition of modern woman must be understood partly in social terms, and that the concept of "genital trauma" has been overdone, see Mirra Komarovsky, *Women in the Modern World: their Education and their Dilemmas* (Boston: Little, Brown and Company, 1953), pp. 31-52.

proving, Komarovsky has shown that the American housewife tends to disparage herself as well as her work, as both being unworthy because they do not receive recognition in terms of cash income.[7]

If woman does not command respect as an earner, she is also likely to incur a certain subtle lack of respect for herself in her role as a consumer. For there is a strong tendency in some phases of American advertising to regard the consumer as someone who may be flattered or may be bullied, but who need not be treated as a mature person. Insofar as the consumer is an object of condescension, someone to be managed rather than someone to be consulted, someone on whom the will of the advertiser is to be imposed by psychological manipulation, and insofar as consumers are primarily women, it means that women become the objects of more than their share of the low esteem in which the consumer is held, and more than their share of the stultifying efforts to play upon human yearnings for prestige and popularity or upon human psychological insecurities. Anyone who recalls the recent publications about the rate at which the blinking of women's eyes increases when they view the display of goods in a supermarket, and the extent to which this display causes them to spend impulsively, rather than according to need, will recognize that the role of the consumer has not enhanced the dignity of women.[8] This aspect was very clearly and wittily recognized by Sylvia Wright in an article in *Harpers* in 1955, in which she dealt ironically with the assertion, which we sometimes hear, that America has become a woman's world.

"Whatever it is," she wrote, "I'll thank you to stop saying it's mine. If it were a woman's world, people wouldn't yammer at me so much. They're always telling me to do, be, or make something. . . .

"The one thing they don't want me to be is me. 'A few drops of Abano Bath Oil' they say, 'and you're not you . . . you're Somebody New lolling in perfumed luxury.' But I'm not allowed to loll long. The next minute I have to spring out in order to be Fire and Ice, swathed in satin, not a thing to do but look stark, and wait for a man to pounce. Turn the page, I've got to make sure it's Johnson's cotton buds with which I swab the baby. A few pages later, the baby gets into the act yelling for fullweight diapers. . . .

[7]Komarovsky, *Woman in the Modern World*, pp. 127-153.

[8]Experiments on the rate of eye-blink, as conducted by James M. Vicary, a leading exponent of motivation research, were reported in Vance Packard, *The Hidden Persuaders* (New York: David McKay Co., 1957), pp. 106-108.

"I'm supposed to use a lot of make-up to keep my husband's love, but I must avoid make-up clog. I'm supposed to be gay, spontaneous and outgoing, but I musn't get 'expression lines' [Expression lines are to wrinkles as morticians are to undertakers.]

"In the old days, I only had to have a natural aptitude for cooking, cleaning, bringing up children, entertaining, teaching Sunday School and tatting . . .

"Now I also have to reconstitute knocked-down furniture and build on porches."[9]

If woman's status is somewhat confused today, therefore, it is partly because, at the very time when efforts to exploit her as a female began to abate, the efforts to exploit her as a consumer began to increase. And at the time when the intrinsic value of her work was gaining in dignity as compared with that of the male, the superficial value as measured in terms of money income was diminishing. The essential strength of her position has increased, but the combined effect of the manipulation by the media and the emphasis upon monetary earning as a standard for the valuation of work has threatened her with a new kind of subordination, imposed by the system of values which she herself accepts, rather than by masculine values imposed upon her against her will.

If a woman as a consumer in a world of producers and as an unpaid worker in a world of salaried employees has lost some of the ground she had gained by emancipation as a female in a world of males, even the emancipation itself has created some new problems for her. For instance, it has confronted her with a dilemma she never faced in the days when she was confined to her own feminine sphere. This is the dilemma that she is now expected to attain a competence in the realm of men's affairs but that she must never succeed in this realm too much. It is well for her to be intelligent, but not intelligent enough to make a young man feel inferior; well for her to find employment and enjoy it, but not enjoy it enough to be unwilling to give it up for the cradle and the sink; well for her to be able to look after herself but never to be so visibly able that it will inhibit the impulse of the right man to want to look after her; well for her to be ambitious, but never ambitious enough actually to put her personal objectives first. When a man marries, no one expects him to cease being a commuter and to become a farmer because it would be good for the children—though in fact it might. But when a woman marries, her occupation becomes an auxiliary activity.

[9]Sylvia Wright, "Whose World? and Welcome to It," in *Harper's Magazine,* vol. 210 (May, 1955), pp. 35-38.

Here we come back to the presence of a fundamental dualism which has made the so-called "emancipation" of women different from the emancipation of any other group in society. Other emancipated groups have sought to substitute a new condition in place of an old one and to obliterate the old, but except for a few of the most militant women in a generation of crusading suffragettes, now almost extinct, women have never renounced the roles of wife and mother. The result has been that their objective was to reconcile a new condition with an old one, to hold in balance the principle of equality, which denies a difference, and the practice of wifehood and motherhood which recognizes a difference in the roles of men and women. The eternal presence of this dualism has not only caused a distressing amount of confusion and tension among women themselves; it has also caused confusion among their many volunteer critics. The result is that we encounter more wildly inconsistent generalizations about modern American women than about almost any other subject.

For example, modern woman, we are told, is gloriously free from the inferiority of the past, but she is miserable and insecure in her new freedom. She wields the purse strings of the nation and has become dominant over a world of increasingly less-masculine men who no longer trust themselves to buy a suit of clothes without their wife's approval. But also she does the routine work at typewriter and sink while the men still run the universe. Similarly, we are assured that the modern woman is an idle, parasitic, bridge-playing victim of technological unemployment in her own mechanized home, and also that she is the busy manager of a family and household and budget whose demands make the domestic chores of the past look easy by comparison. She escapes from reality into the wretched, petty little world of soap opera and neighborhood gossip, but she excels in her knowledge of public affairs and she became an effective guardian of literary and artistic values when her money-grubbing husband defaulted on the responsibility. She is rearing the best crop of children ever produced on this planet, by the most improved methods ever devised, while her over-protectiveness has bred "momism" and her unwillingness to stay at home has bred delinquency.

VIII

Clearly, we are still a long way from having arrived at any monotonous unanimity of opinion about the character of American women. Yet if we will focus carefully upon what we really know with some degree of assurance, we can perhaps begin the process of striking a balance. We certainly know, for instance, that many of the trends of American history have been operative for both men and women in somewhat the same way. The emphasis upon the right of the individual has operated to remove legal disabilities upon women, to open many avenues to gainful employment, to confer the suffrage, and so on. Even our divorce rate is an ironic tribute to the fact that the interests of the individual, and perhaps in a majority of cases the individual woman, are placed ahead of the protection of a social institution—namely the family. The rejection of authority in American life, which has made our child-rearing permissive and has weakened the quality of leadership in our politics, has also meant that the relation of husband and wife is more of a partnership and less of an autocracy in this age and in this country than at any other time or place in Western civilization. The competitive strain in American life has impelled American women as well as American men to strive hard for their goals, and to assert themselves in the strife—indeed European critics complain that they assert themselves far more strenuously than European women and entirely too much for the tranquility of society.

On the other hand, we also know that the experience of women remains in many ways a distinctive experience. Biologically, there are still the age-old facts that women are not as big as men and not as strong; that the sex act involves consequences for them which it does not involve for the male; that the awareness of these consequences conditions the psychological attitudes of women very deeply; and that motherhood is a biological function while fatherhood is, in a sense, a cultural phenomenon. Historically, there is the formidable truth that the transformations of modern life have impinged upon men and women in different ways. The avenues of employment opened to men are not the same as the avenues of employment opened to women. The revolution in our economy has deepened the division between work in the home and work outside the home by according the sanction of monetary reward to the one and denying it to the other—thus devaluing in a new way work which is distinctively woman's. The economic revolution, while converting most men from producers to earners, has converted most women from processors to consumers, and the exploitation of the consumer has, again, added a new devaluation to woman's role. Society has given her the opportunity to fulfill her personal ambitions through the same career-activities as a man, but it cannot make her career aspirations and her family aspirations fit together as they do for a man. The result of all this is a certain tension between her old role and her new one. More of an individualist than women in traditional societies, she is by no means as whole-heartedly individualistic as the American male, and as a study at Berkeley recently showed, she still hesitates to claim individualism as a quality of her own.[10] If she enters the competitive race, she does so with an awareness that the top posts are still pretty much the monopoly of men, and with a certain limitation upon her competitive commitment. In short, she is constantly holding in balance her general opportunities as a person and her distinctive needs as a woman, and when we consider how badly these two go together in principle, can we not say that she is maintaining the operative equilibrium between them with a remarkable degree of skill and of success?

The answer to my childish riddle was that the big Indian is the little Indian's mother. To say that she is a squaw is not to deny that she is an Indian—but it is to say that she is an Indian for whom the expectations of the masculine world of Indians, or of Americans, do not apply. It is to say that her qualities and traits, whether she is an Indian, or an American, will reflect the influence of the same sweeping forces which influence the world of men, but that it will reflect them with a difference. In this sense, what we say about the character of the American people should be said not in terms of half of the American population—even if it is the male half—but in terms of the character of the totality of the people. In this sense, also, attention to the historic character of American women is important not only as a specialty for female scholars or for men who happen to take an interest in feminism, but as a coordinate major part of the over-all, comprehensive study of the American character as a whole. For the character of any nation is the composite of the character of its men and of its women and though these may be deeply similar in many ways, they are almost never entirely the same.

---

[10] John P. McKee and A. C. Sheriffs, "Men's and Women's Beliefs, Ideals, and Self-Concepts," in *American Journal of Sociology*, LXIV (1959), pp. 356-363.

HENRY JAMES AND CHILDHOOD:
THE TURN OF THE SCREW

By ALBERT E. STONE, JR.

Albert E. Stone, Jr. is a graduate of the American Studies program at Yale University. He is Professor and Chairman of the English department at Emory University in Atlanta, Georgia. He is the author of THE INNOCENT EYE: CHILDHOOD IN MARK TWAIN'S IMAGINATION and the editor of Crèvecoeur's LETTERS FROM AN AMERICAN FARMER and SKETCHES OF XVIII-CENTURY AMERICA.

"But ah, the exposure indeed, the helpless plasticity of childhood that isn't dear or sacred to somebody! That was my little tragedy!"
JAMES TO DR. LOUIS WALDSTEIN, 1898

The scene has stamped itself upon our imaginations. A young governess awakens one night in a big English country-house to discover that her two beautiful little charges, Miles and Flora, are not in their beds. Gliding silently and breathlessly through the dim rooms of Bly she comes first upon Flora, face pressed to the pane, peering out into the garden. At another window the governess herself looks into the night. There on the moon-flooded terrace stands Miles. He is gazing raptly up at the house. But the boy is not looking either at his sister's or the governess's window, to see if his nocturnal prank is detected and appreciated; he is looking above the governess's head, up at the old tower of Bly. There, the governess feels sure, stands Peter Quint, the dead man-servant whose ghost has returned to claim Miles and Flora as his own. The chain, then, originates with the governess who watches Flora who watches Miles who watches the ghost on the tower. It is a circuit connecting young and old, innocent and corrupt, living and dead, perhaps even the sane and the insane. But who is who? The mystery of *The Turn of the Screw* is caught and crystallized in the complex pattern of words of which, like all fictional art, the literary image is composed.

Literature is a matter of effective images, and this particular one has tingled the spines of a large number of Americans since its initial appearance in the pages of *Collier's Weekly* in the spring of 1898. Unlike many of the elaborate embroideries in prose which James published during the later years of his long career, this tale has always been popular, with critics and with the common reader. One reason for this, of course, is that ghost stories possess a perennial appeal. Furthermore, the presence of a child gives in this case, as the narrator points out, "another turn of the screw" to the atmosphere of horror; and this story contains not one child but several. For if Miles and Flora personify childish beauty and defenselessness, the young governess is innocence itself, and even Mrs. Grose, the simple, illiterate housekeeper, is essentially a childlike figure. Four children in all are left alone to confront the ghosts at Bly. James has brought off something which even our master Gothicist Edgar Allen Poe did not attempt—the mating of a mystery story with a classic study of childish innocence and its involvement with corruption.

This acievement not only won *The Turn of the Screw*'s author an unwonted popular reception, it reaffirmed his connection with a tradition in American fiction, already well established by the 1890's, of writing about childhood. Miles, Flora, and the governess take their places beside Pearl and Ilbrahim, Phoebe Pyncheon and the Snow Maiden, Tom Sawyer and Huckleberry Finn, Daisy Miller and Nanda Brookenham, Joan of Arc and Maggie Johnson and the others in the cast of juvenile characters which during the nineteenth century was so conspicuously an American contribution to world literature. James added his cosmopolitan voice to the more indigenous accents of his master Hawthorne and his contemporaries Mark Twain and Stephen Crane in a national invocation to innocence and immaturity.

Instead of expressing—like most European writers, thinkers, and artists—cultural values and preoccupations associated with mature, adult, social life, James now appeared to join those who celebrated quite opposite norms. Purity as inexperience, intelligence as simplicity and intuition, behavior as solitude or withdrawal, the moral directness of the innocent eye of youth—this was the constellation of values asserted, albeit often ambiguously or ironically, in such works of the American imagination as "The Gentle Boy," *The Scarlet Letter, Tom Sawyer, The Prince and the Pauper, Huckleberry Finn,* and *Maggie, A Girl of the Streets.* James himself contributed *Daisy Miller,* "The Pupil," *What Maisie Knew,* and *The Awkward Age* to the emerging image of American Adam as adolescent.

One of the clearest ways in which *The Turn of the Screw* shares this tradition is through its principal actors. During the sixty-odd years following Hawthorne's "The Gentle Boy" (which in 1832 became the first piece of serious childhood fiction in America), the cast of childish characters assumed a formal, almost stereotyped identity. There developed at least three recognizable juvenile roles —the precocious infant (Hawthorne's Pearl or Elsie), the Bad Boy (Aldrich's Tom Bailey, Tom Sawyer), and the virginal maiden (Phoebe Pyncheon or Crane's Maggie).

Flora, Miles, and their governess are cut from the same three bolts of cloth. "Young as she was," the governess tells us of Flora at their first meeting. "I was struck, throughout our little tour, with her confidence and courage, . . . her disposition to tell me so many more things than she asked." The little girl's later conduct fulfills this promise of preternatural knowledge and aplomb; in many respects she is a reincarnation of Hester Prynne's child. The governess, on the other hand, appears quite traditionally, as *less* mature and sophisticated than her twenty years. The "youngest of several daughters of a poor country parson," she is a "fluttered, anxious" beginner in the schoolroom, as "young, untried, nervous" as Phoebe Pyncheon on her first day at the House of the Seven Gables. Little Miles, for all his suavity and good manners, is not unlike a British cousin of Tom Sawyer. "When I'm bad I *am* bad!" he confesses gaily after the midnight escapade. Like any normal boy (which he may, after all, be), Miles chafes under petticoat government and wants "what a boy wants!"

The plot pattern, too, of these American stories of childhood became in some respects as formalized as the character roles. What traditionally *happens* to the precocious infant, the Bad Boy, or the virginal maiden is some sudden and violent introduction to the world of grownups, a world discovered to be either ambiguously or flagrantly evil. Modern anthropologists would term this initiation experience "the rites of passage." For Pearl in *The Scarlet Letter* the moments of illumination occur on the scaffold. In the case of Tom Sawyer, it is the harrowing brush with death in the cave. Huck Finn's initiation is more difficult to define; in a sense, the vagabond boy has always known the worst about human nature; but the various forays ashore from the raft appreciably widen and deepen Huck's awareness of the personal and social evil that threatens his and Jim's world.

To be sure, the adolescent's arrival at maturity which the word "passage" implies does not invariably take place. Pearl is transformed by her father's death, but neither Tom nor Huck nor Henry Fleming quite live up to the moral opportunities forced upon them in the cave, or the river, or on the battlefield. Either they do not *see* the significance of events, or else having seen, they renounce, as Huck does in the Evasion at Uncle Silas's farm, the moral vision so hardly won.

In spite of lapses, however, it is the quality of a young person's moral insight that is the keynote of many nineteenth-century American novels. Again and again, a boy or girl points the accusing finger at the adult world's moral spots. "Thou wast not bold! —thou wast not true." Pearl cries to her weakwilled father in the forest. "Aunt Polly, it ain't fair," says Tom Sawyer to the assembled grown-ups at the funeral reunion. "Somebody's got to be glad to see Huck." And Huck Finn's declaration of moral independence is the most agonizingly honest one of all. "All right, then, I'll *go* to hell," rings in our ears as a clearer, pithier condemnation of slavery than all the histrionics of *Uncle Tom's Cabin.*

Because of the foreign setting and an unusual and overpowering aura of suspense and horror which distinguished *The Turn of the Screw,* Jame's tale does not at first display the affinity which it actually possesses with *The Scarlet Letter* or the novels of Mark Twain. Not only is a representative cast assembled at Bly, but something like a traditional initiation is taking place there. Innocence demonstrates its perception of, and opposition to, the depravity incarnated in the ghosts of Peter Quint and Miss Jessel. At the end, the malignant spirits are presumably routed, but the simple governess' world has been turned upside down and little Miles is dead.

This ironic, even tragic dénouement contrasts sharply with the tidier outcomes of previous childish encounters with adult sinfulness in the writings of James's fellow Americans. Furthermore, this different conclusion is a piece with James's deliberately confusing presentation of character, motive, and value judgment that differentiates *The Turn of the Screw* from other stories of childhood. The easy thing to say, of course, is that such characteristics are generic to the ghost story. But there are, I think, more fundamental questions at issue than simply the techniques of mystification. James has written, we must grant, a story that contains the ingredients of a conventional American exploration of childhood. But the final imprint that remains in the sensitive reader's mind is so murky and indeterminate that it must be more than the fault of the ghosts. Perhaps Henry James, in 1898, took this oblique way

of disagreeing with his contemporaries about the value of innocence, about the significance of a child's violent immersion in adult
affairs, and about the nature and worth of moral insight based on
ignorance and inexperience, no matter how pure and blameless.
These are at least some relevant questions which might be directed
at the little "pot-boiler" and *"jeu d'esprit,"* as James once deprecat-
ingly called *The Turn of the Screw.* However, as Douglas, the
narrator, pointedly warns, we are not necessarily to expect clear
answers to such queries. "The story *won't* tell," he remarks to the
curious group around the fireside, "not in any literal, vulgar way."

II

Since the fabric *is* deceptive, one might best begin to unmask
the meanings of *The Turn of the Screw* by establishing the kind of
"reality" James presupposes for his tale. By this I mean, for one
thing, the inescapably mysterious quality of the events narrated.
Though in a famous letter to H. G. Wells James wrote of his trying for "absolute lucidity and logic" in the governess's account,[1]
it is obvious that the "singleness of effect" actually achieved is
that of unsolved and unsolvable enigmas. No matter how carefully
we read and reason we shall never settle all doubts about the events,
about the children, about the governess's sanity. As for the "reality"
of the ghosts themselves, we must, I feel accept the governess's
word. They exist for her so they must exist for the reader. As Mary
McCarthy has recently written, "The narrator is, precisely, an eye-
witness, testifying to the reader that these things really happened,
even though the reader knows of course that they did not."[2] The
supernatural is a necessary part of the world at Bly as it is at
Elsinore.

We must not, to be sure, limit ourselves to the perspective of
the young girl who relates her battle with the phantoms. A further
aspect of the tale's reality—and this is something that the governess
does not realize—is the sense of evil pervading everything. Corruption is clearly in the ghosts and may have infected Flora and Miles,
but there are other and more subtle forms of iniquity abroad. Evil
has tainted the thoughts and actions of the children's companion
and even of the good housekeeper. It also exists in the world beyond
Bly. The master in Harley Street bears a share of the general evil

---

[1]See Leon Edel, ed., *The Selected Letters of Henry James* (New York,
1960), p. 146.

[2]Mary McCarthy, "The Fact in Fiction," *Partisan Review* XXVII, No. 3
(Summer, 1960), p. 451.

which the young lady finds in the ghosts but which the reader sees not merely in Quint but as omnipresent. Just as, in willing suspension of disbelief, one accepts the spirits, so ought we to acknowledge the pervasive miasma of sin in this story. Like any work of art, *The Turn of the Screw* enacts its own rules of reality.

Furthermore, James's story, despite special supernatural qualities that appear to set it apart, does in fact bear a distinct relationship to the author's other novels and stories. This is a literary truism often overlooked in the spate of criticism which has all but inundated *The Turn of the Screw* during the last thirty years.[3] In particular, Miles and Flora's story has links with the novels and stories about children which James wrote in the Nineties. During this period (marked in another area by his distastrously unsuccessful attempts at playwriting) James devoted a major part of his imaginative powers to this facet of experience. Before that time, American innocence—especially as plentifully endowed with money and confronted by European cupidity and baseness—had been Henry James's special theme, but except for *Daisy Miller* (1878) and a few smaller pieces like "The Author of Beltraffio" (1884), his innocents had not been children. But with "The Pupil" early in the decade and in *What Maisie Knew* and *The Awkward Age* James turned deliberately to the exploration of European society as seen from the children's quarters. The moral worth of the sophisticated members of English and continental aristocracy, as well as that of some expatriate Americans, was measured through the innocent eyes of their children.

The result is a wholesale arraignment. James's rich, self-indul-

---

[3]For a representative but by no means exhaustive collection of essays, see Gerald Willen, ed., *A Casebook on Henry James's The Turn of the Screw* (New York, 1960). In addition to the text of the story and James's own Preface, this volume reprints the following articles: Edna Kenton, "Henry James to the Ruminant Reader: The Turn of the Screw"; Edmund Wilson, "The Ambiguity of Henry James"; Nathan Bryllion Fagin, "Another reading of *The Turn of the Screw*"; A Radio Symposium: Katherine Anne Porter, Allen Tate, Mark Van Doren, "James: The Turn of the Screw"; A. J. A. Waldock, "Mr. Edmund Wilson and *The Turn of the Screw*"; Robert Heilman, "*The Turn of the Screw* as Poem"; Glenn A Reed, "Another Turn on James' 'The Turn of the Screw' "; Oliver Evans, "James's Air of Evil: *The Turn of the Screw*"; Charles Hoffmann, "Innocence and Evil in James's *The Turn of the Screw*"; Oscar Cargill, "Henry James as Freudian Pioneer"; John Silver, "A note on the Freudian Reading of *The Turn of the Screw*"; Harold C. Goddard, "A Pre-Freudian Reading of *The Turn of the Screw*"; John Lydenburg, "The Governess Turns the Screws"; Joseph J. Firebaugh, "Inadequacy in Eden: Knowledge and *The Turn of the Screw*"; Alexander E. Jones, "Point of View in *The Turn of the Screw*." One additional essay of considerable insight might be added: Donald P. Costello, "The Structure of *The Turn of the Screw*," *Modern Language Notes*, LXXV, No. 4 (April, 1960), pp. 312-321.

gent parents, too preoccupied with pleasure, social status, money, or sexual intrigue to bother with their offspring, stand condemned for their abuse of innocence. As for the beautiful, perceptive, reticent girls and boys—Maisie Farrange, Nanda Brookenham, Morgan Moreen, and the others—their fate is to languish in isolation or to be tossed like shuttlecocks from one indifferent adult to another. Between parents and children stands usually one devoted person, a tutor (like Morgan's Pemberton), a nurse (like Maisie's Mrs. Wix), or a governess, who remains true to a trust that all too often goes unappreciated and unpaid. An essential part, too, of the pathetic situation is the uncovering of a tragic limitation, either of intelligence or will-power or of financial resources, on the part of the child's would-be protector which makes defeat for both of them inevitable. As a consequence, each of these works chronicles the victimization of childhood.

The Turn of the Screw is precisely a tale of this sort. The master in Harley Street stands *in loco parentis* to Flora and Miles, and his instructions to the governess—"she should never trouble him—but never, never: only meet all questions herself, receive all moneys from his solicitor, take the whole thing over and let him alone"—betray his kinship to the Farranges, the Brookenhams, and the Moreens. As for the governess, she does not, like Pemberton of "The Pupil," suffer from too little love of her charge (she errs, perhaps, in the opposite direction), nor is she limited in mind and imagination as Mrs. Wix. But there is abundant evidence that her egotism and rigid middle-class morality are weak weapons with which to fight Peter Quint. In the final scene, at any rate, Miles lies dead, even though his little heart has been "dispossessed" as a result of the governess's valiant, unavailing fight.

There is no doubt that James himself regarded his ghostly tale as linked to these other works by the theme of innocence betrayed. In the summer of 1898, the author made this comment in a letter to Dr. Louis Waldstein: "But ah, the exposure indeed, the helpless plasticity of childhood that isn't dear or sacred to *somebody!* That *was* my little tragedy!" This statement points to one of the major motifs running through *The Turn of the Screw*. The key words here are "dear" and "sacred." Both terms draw attention away from psychopathological and metaphysical questions (legitimate and important as these are) and toward the social, moral, and religious dimensions of the story.

These are, it seems to me, aspects of a literary artifact of the greatest interest to cultural historians. For it is the writer and his work in their relation to culture and to historical problems of value arising in that culture which chiefly concern the literary critic when he dons an American Studies cap. In this instance, James's use of "dear" and "sacred" suggests value judgments arising from stress felt between certain social institutions (like the family) and traditional Christian ideology. Something is seriously wrong with a social order, James is suggesting, that allows and encourages the betrayal of an innocence deemed sacrosanct by its own religion.

Insofar as *The Turn of the Screw* dramatizes the exposure and plasticity of childhood it ceases to be simply a mystery story and becomes a social document. I would go further and assert that *The Turn of the Screw* is "about" the problem of social class stratification and the religious psychology of a person occupying a peculiarly vulnerable but important position in that social system. This is, of course, a gross oversimplification. Like all formulas, it omits a great deal. But if, recognizing this, we proceed to such positive insights as the comment may contain, it may be possible to throw fresh light on what surely is the most shadowy and elusive short story of modern literature.

III

How can any revelation of evil as largely sociological compare with ghosts or an insane governess or diabolical children as an emotionally satisfactory image of horror? The answer is obvious; none can. To admit this is to establish at once the limits of intellectualizing a ghost story in the manner I suggest. But horror has its vogues and fashions like any other human response. What could raise the genteel hackles of James's readers in 1898 may no longer prove so effective. Indeed, there appear to be several reasons why the reader of 1960 finds it difficult to respond emotionally to the atmosphere of *The Turn of the Screw* in the same manner as the previous two generations. For one thing, our age is familiar with some new forms of the supernatural which render apparitions or hallucinations tamer devices than they once were. I refer not only to our familiarity with abnormal psychology, but also to such experiments as those of Dr. Rhine on extrasensory perception; others might include flying saucers or the alleged achievements of the ouija board, Madam Blavatsky, or the Society for Psychic Research. Furthermore, the twentieth century has grown rather blasé about matters of sexual perversion with which the story of Miles and Peter Quint is unmistakably infused. Most important of all, perhaps, is the fact that the present day reader is far less excited than he once was by intimations of human depravity and corruption. We know too much for sure on this score to respond as we once did to hints. There is no doubt that Hiroshima and Buchenwald have made it harder to read *The Turn of the Screw.*

I do not deny the power of James's prose to arouse and control feeling. But for us to regard the tale as anything more than simply a scary story we must be able to feel the evil in *The Turn of the Screw* as actual and necessary to the events—"actual" in the sense that a verifiable social and psychological situation is being adumbrated, "necessary" because the story could not be told apart from the conditions James presents. What makes Henry James superior as a mystery writer, to, say, August Derleth or John Collier, is this huge substream of social fact underlying his images of terror.

The Turn of the Screw portrays a nineteenth-century society organized so as to make victimization almost inevitable for children in the situation of Miles and Flora. Bly itself is the symbol of the English social order. "Wasn't it just a storybook over which I had fallen a-doze and a-dream?" muses the ingenuous, perceptive governess at the close of her first day. "No; it it was a big, ugly, antique, but convenient house embodying a few features of a building still older, half replaced and half utilised, in which I had the fancy of our being almost as lost as a handful of passengers in a great drifting ship." One does not need to be familiar with Jame's use elsewhere of house-and-garden imagery, as in *The Portrait of a Lady,* to see that Bly is not simply a gentleman's country-seat but represents also hierarchy itself, a "big, ugly, antique, but convenient" institution. The drifting ship metaphor, so far from vitiating this intimation, further reinforces the notion of the house as microcosm of a society lacking proper control and moral responsibility.

There are at Bly but two aristocrats, for the actual master resolutely remains in London, enforcing his hands-off policy. As the governess sees them, Miles and Flora are "a pair of little grandees" or "princes of the blood" abandoned to the care of a staff of servants. At the head of and distinctly above these lower orders, but demonstrably below her grandees, is the governess. She stands at the very fulcrum of the social tensions with which the story is filled. (A vicar's daughter, as Lloyd Warner or any sociologist would attest, is an ideal observer of social class.) Through her, we become acutely conscious not only of selfish irresponsibility at the top but of the reticent, conscious superiority of the two lovely children and of the mute humility of Mrs. Grose. We also sense the governess's own reserve and social timidity in her dealings with Miles and Flora. We gradually learn how Peter Quint, when he was alive, manipulated the class situation to his licentious ends. Comprehending all these various manifestations is the overwhelming fact of communication between classes at Bly as strained, formal, incomplete. Even the governess's love cannot make it otherwise.

One of Henry James's special marks as artist is his knack of suggesting obliquely, succinctly, but unmistakably a whole series of perceptions within a short scene or, indeed, paragraph. A notable instance of this symbolizing skill, illustrating James at his best as social commentator, occurs when, on their way to church one Sunday morning, the governess makes this observation to herself about young Miles at her side: "Turned out for Sunday by his uncle's tailor, who had had a free hand and a notion of pretty waistcoats and of his grand little air, Miles's whole title to independence, the rights of his sex and situation, were so stamped upon him that if he had suddenly struck for freedom I should have had nothing to say." This brief comment, ostensibly about clothing, touches almost every manifestation of wrong already hinted at in the narrative. Clothes, of course, are to be taken no more casually in James's world than architecture or manners; each can be endowed with profound implications. Here the reference to waistcoats recalls at once Peter Quint, his peculiar pretensions, and his corrupting influence. In the first conversation between Mrs. Grose and the governess (after the ghost's initial appearance on the tower), Quint's history and character are revealed in a series of questions and answers having to do with social appearance. "He has no hat." . . . "He never wore his hat, but he did wear—well, there were waistcoats missed!" . . . "A gentleman?" gasped Mrs. Grose, "confounded, stupified: a gentleman *he?*" Miles's debonair appearance then, may derive not from innocent, embellished beauty but from a tailor's "free hand" (the master is always giving some servant a free hand with his dead brother's children) and from the example of another waistcoat-fancier. Thus a fond, innocuous remark assumes sinister overtones, just as the boy's "grand little air" may now be a similarly deceiving description of duplicity.

His demands for freedom, too, can no longer appear simply as boyish impatience; they hint at licentious revolt, conditioned by "sex and situation," against the governess's moral restraint. But, again, is not Miles's "title to independence" a valid one? Might not the sexual aggressor (if there is one) be unconsciously the living companion and not the dead one? Each of these innuendoes is wrapped in the language, so to speak, of a society columnist reporting a scene. This reporter, however, is a young girl from the provinces, very much on the defensive before the waistcoat and what it represents.

Another essential ingredient of the mystery and horror of this tale consists of words and confidences that are *not* spoken. Conversations in *The Turn of the Screw* are always skirting "forbidden ground." This helps immeasurably to thicken the dramatic atmosphere, throwing as it does so much weight on the frantic imaginings of the twenty-year-old girl. But secrets and silences, useful as they are for ghostly effect, often originate in the social relation of superior and subordinate, whereby confidences may go downward but not up. "There were things enough, taking one with another, to chatter about," she remarks at one point of the children, "if one went very fast and knew by instinct when to go around. They pulled with an art of their own the strings of my invention and my memory; and nothing else perhaps, when I thought of such occasions afterwards, gave me so the suspicion of being watched from under cover. It was in any case over *my* life, *my* past, and *my* friends alone that we could take anything like our ease. . . ." The conspicuous reticence of these charming small aristocrats effectively stifles the "monstrous utterance of words" that would bring the ghosts and their corruption out into the open. But as these gross questions "died away on my lips," the governess reports, "I said to myself that I should indeed help them to represent something infamous, if by pronouncing them, I should violate as rare a little case of instinctive delicacy as any schoolroom, probably, had ever known. When I said to myself: '*they* have the manners to be silent, and you, trusted as you are, the baseness to speak!' " The ironic freight which the words "delicacy" and "manners" is made to bear here is considerable, as James makes vividly clear later when little Flora loses her patrician secretiveness and goes to pieces in a flood of filthy invective. Miles alone keeps his aristocratic guard up until the very last minute.

I trust no one has received the impression from these summary quotations and comments on the sociological aspect of *The Turn of the Screw* that the story can be reduced to this dimension or that James, in some simple-minded American way, intended a wholesale condemnation of social class. His sense of the complexity of human experience and motive is, I trust, sufficiently obvious to destroy both simplifications. By the tale's end it is equally clear that the governess has been both the instrument and object of exploration; we see through her as we see the events unfolding through her eyes. The narrative exposes both her insights and insecurities, her perceptions of the situation and her involvement in it. If the ghosts are in one sense her personifications of past and present social iniquity at Bly they have also been magnified and distorted by her ignorance, given a sexual twist by her infatuation with the master and by her middle-class taboos. Her all-too-human vision of evil is then forced violently and prematurely upon little Miles in the final, fatal confrontation with the ghost of Quint. The boy's death, consequently, is both her fault and that of the system which permits the abuse of childhood. It may, of course, also be Miles's own fault.

IV

To return for a moment to Miles in his pretty waistcoat; it is not, I think, a coincidence that the party at Bly is on the way to church. The phrase "turned out for Sunday" points to a religious—indeed, Christian—side to *The Turn of the Screw,* one apparent to every reader, and a dimension that Robert Heilman has examined brilliantly in *"The Turn of the Screw* as Poem." To approach this matter from the angle of clothing and social behavior, however, puts it into a somewhat different perspective from that most critics have employed. That viewpoint is heavily ironic, for the religious problem which James dramatizes is as much a personal as a universal parable; it is one of individual shortcomings, idiosyncracies, and eventual failure. Miles's death must be accepted as a defeat for the forces of righteousness; for the causes of catastrophe for the child lie so clearly in his governess's theory and practice of Christianity that any theological view of the tale as a modern morality play, a latter-day version of the Fall, must also consider the social psychology of the Christians involved.

For this purpose, as for the illumination of class tensions, James's choice of an immature vicar's daughter as actor-narrator was a brilliant one. There is, first of all, the religious vocabulary that falls so naturally from her lips. "I had an absolute certainty that I could see again what I had already seen," she remarks early in the story, "but something within me said that by offering myself bravely as the sole subject of such experience, by accepting, by inviting, by surmounting it all, I should serve as an expiatory victim and guard the tranquillity of my companions. The children, in especial, I should thus fence about and absolutely save." These brave words do not, as it turns out, do the trick. This is not to say that James mocks the girl's self-sacrifice, but he does employ the Biblical imagery with heavy ambiguity. The governess imagines herself "an expiatory victim" assuring salvation for her threatened innocents, the "angels," the "holy infants." The ghost of Quint, to her mind, is the Devil himself invading Bly-Eden with his "poison." Her own role, as this Miltonic vocabulary suggests, is more than a "sister of Charity" or a saint; it is closer to the atonement of Christ.

For an inexperienced young girl to cast herself so confidently in the guise of savior inevitably raises questions both as to the adequacy of her formulations of the evil she fights and the quality of her own spiritual life. On each count the weakness of her mere unaided innocence is implied. Though Professor Heilman believes she has "an inquiring lay mind with a religious sense but without precise theological tools," I see the governess rather as a child bravely but mistakenly grappling with a problem she does not comprehend. Hence much of the responsibility—and this tale is at heart a study of responsibility—for Miles's fatal "dispossession" must be laid to the governess's insistent over-simplification of evil. Hers is a religious imagination that defines iniquity as an either-or condition. One is either pure or vile, never a human mixture. Thus the language of her naive dualism converts Flora at one bound from "angel" to "demon." As for the boy, "If Miles is innocent, what, then, am *I*?" is her instinctive query to Mrs. Grose when doubts begin to assail them.

This doctrinaire outlook stems, as Joseph Firebaugh has pointed out, from the governess's almost frantic fear lest her little charges learn too much about life. To her black-and-white mind, Quint's influence on Miles has not been merely permissively lax; instead, "the imagination of all evil *had* been opened up to him." If the boy is allowed to go off to another school (the obvious symbol of knowledge) he will simply be "turned out again" with more "bravado" and "dishonor" on his little head. Far better, then, to remain innocently and, if need be, ignorantly within the park-grounds. Such a cruelly narrow vision of childish development marks the final scene with special irony, for when the phantom appears for the last time at "the haunted pane" he is "a sentinel before a prison." May not Miles's desperate search for a way out of the prison of Bly mean that the governess and not the ghost is his warden? It is she who has sought to suppress the child's natural desire to see the world. Like Jo March in *Little Women,* she appears to long for flat-irons to put on the heads of her charges to keep them from growing up. Her whole philosophy of time slips out within a pair of parentheses when she observes, "(for all futures are rough!)."

On herself, however, the governess imposes no such limits to the knowledge of corruption. Like Oedipus, "a dreadful boldness of mind" urges her to uncover every secret. "But I shall get it out of you yet!" is her cry to poor timid Mrs. Grose. To herself she confesses, "all the justice within me ached for the proof that it [Miles's imagination of all evil] could ever have flowered into an act." Like Oedipus, too, the young guardian at Bly exhibits at times *hubris* so boundless that even the disclosure of Flora's depraved vocabulary is welcomed because it "so justifies" her suspicions. But though the girl shares with the Greeks a belief in "absolute intelligence," she never, within the narrative at least, achieves that spiritual humility before the gods which would make her a genuinely religious person. She can perhaps unravel the Sphinx's riddle of original sin but she never arrives at Colonus.

In fact, the governess never gets inside a church. "Oh, I'm not fit for church!" she wails after glimpsing the ghost, and this remark, like almost everything in this remarkable tale, has its ironies. Though she yearns for "the almost spiritual help of the hassock" during the crucial interview with Miles in the churchyard, it is not to God she turns. Indeed, this girl never once prays. Any impartial appraisal of her spiritual life would find her neither contrite, nor merciful nor joyous nor trusting in divine power.

Her religion instead is an absolutist love of purity that issues in blind truth-seeking and insistence upon innocence at any price. In mistaken devotion to this rigid creed she sacrifices Flora almost gladly and even, reluctantly, Miles. Hers is a shallow and dangerous Christianity that by turns sentimentalizes and derogates the innocence of youth. Yet the melancholy fact is that this naive girl is the only conscience, the sole moral imagination in the tale. For everyone else at Bly, religion consists simply of proper Sunday attire, walks through the park to Evensong, and the day off. As a consequence, there exists in the world of *The Turn of the Screw* no moral force adequately and maturely able to arm the governess's defence of childhood against the depravities and laxities of a secular order. This is the pathetic but unavoidable conclusion we are forced to when we accept Bly as the image of an actual nineteenth-century society with real people in it as well as ghosts.

V

The common reader who has read and reread, with growing perplexity, *The Turn of the Screw* and even followed some of the critics through the winding maze of words they have constructed about the tale, may well conclude by throwing up his hands. After all, he has an invitation to dismiss the work from Henry James;

"it is a piece of ingenuity pure and simple," he wrote in the Preface to the collected works, "of cold artistic calculation, an *amusette* to catch those not easily caught (the 'fun' of the capture of the merely witless being ever but small), the jaded, the disillusioned, the fastidious." If the author himself admits to having composed nothing more serious than an *amusette* to "catch" blasé readers of *Collier's Weekly,* what possible use, then, can this ghost story serve for students of American culture? Can a piece of fiction so filled with calculated irony and ambiguity, artfully designed to pull the reader's leg, tell *anything* about James's world of 1898? These are legitimate queries which raise the larger issue of art's function in cultural history, of which *The Turn of the Screw* is but an exaggerated instance.

There is no doubt that humor, irony, hyperbole, and all the other modulations of tone and mode available to the novelist distort what the historian or sociologist would call the content of his work. But they do not destroy it, any more than the writer's individuality and the privacy of his utterance destroy the essential publicness of his book. All artists—even Emily Dickinson behind her father's hedge in Amherst or Ezra Pound behind the bars at St. Elizabeth's—play a triple role. They are of necessity the creatures, creators, and critics of their culture. Henry James is no exception, though certain allowances must be made for his Anglo-American outlook.

In the case of *The Turn of the Screw,* for instance, we may not take his parable of aristocratic family life (or absence thereof) as applying necessarily to the United States. But the author *is* American-born, writing for an American magazine audience, and with marked success. He chooses children as actors and childhood as theme, and thus, consciously or not, connects himself to an American literary tradition. The task of the historian of culture becomes that of distinguishing James's contribution to that running dialogue about innocence carried on by his fellow American writers during the greater part of the nineteenth century.

Stated in the refreshing idiom of Leslie Fiedler, *The Turn of the Screw* signals an end to Wordsworth and Jean Jacques Rousseau. So far from continuing to celebrate the innocent eye of youth as moral norm, James dramatizes, through his precocious infant, his Bad Boy, and above all, through his virginal maiden, the inadequacies and dangers of inexperience and immaturity. After a century of sentimentality, this ghost story asserts with deadly seriousness the presence of original sin in the minds of the very young. Of course, James does not deny the beauty of innocence. It is of the very essence of this story that the tensions between the two never relax. As the governess observes of the ghosts' influence on Miles and Flora, "they've made them—their two friends, I mean—still cleverer even than nature did; for it was wondrous material to play on!" This, in a nutshell, is the tragic insight of *The Turn of the Screw.*

To be merely innocent is no longer a condition worth venerating by adults. But to be bereft of innocence in the sudden, violent fashion of Miles and his governess is equally tragic—and, in a morally-aware society, unnecessary. The searing scene of Miles's dispossession is dramatically and emotionally needed, but part of its delayed impact is the reader's realization that socially and psychologically such moral experiences are neither necessary nor desirable. They are, in fact, disastrous. Without directly mentioning it, James sets the reader to imagining counter-versions of adult-child relations, like, for instance, Horace Bushnell's notions of Christian nurture, in which childhood is protected against its own innocence and sinfullness and gradually introduced to the meaning of moral maturity. For the reader of 1964, at any rate, these are legitimate implications to be drawn from James's fairy-tale and ones that set *The Turn of the Screw* off from, and criticize, other American versions of initiation experience.

Does not James, too, redefine nineteenth-century platitudes about the moral imagination of childhood? Without losing admiration for the governess's pluck or sympathy for Mile's wavering allegiance to corruption, one is made to see how fatally much children and adolescents *cannot* see. Not that adults in *The Turn of the Screw* are more aware; Mrs. Grose and Peter Quint each, in opposite ways, are inferior moralists to Miles' and Flora's companion. There is on this score, James asserts, no qualitative or guaranteed difference between young and old. It is the author's tactic, however, to explode the contrary myth by pretending to honor it. In the process James revises what in earlier writers had all too frequently been sentimental or false values. More significantly, he prepares the way in the twentieth century for writers like Hemingway, Faulkner, Eudora Welty, and Salinger, carriers of the tradition of writing about childhood's "primal unwarped world" that for a century and a quarter has been one distinguishing mark of our national letters. In this history the little *amusette* Henry James wrote plays a more central role than its sly author may have foreseen. For *The Turn of the Screw,* despite all ambiguities, pays childhood the ultimate tribute of taking it with utter seriousness.

PART  FOUR

Two Underlying Forces:
Technology and Democracy

TECHNOLOGY IN AMERICAN CULTURE

by MORRELL HEALD

Morrell Heald is Associate Professeor of History at Case Institute of Technology in Cleveland, Ohio. He is the author of numerous articles dealing with the role of business and technology in American society. He is currently completing a book dealing with the idea of the social responsibility of business in the United States.

What is the promise of technology for America today? And under what circumstances, likely or unlikely, is that promise capable of achievement? On the one hand, we hear that science and technology make possible levels of leisure and material well-being without precedent except in the most utopian of dreams. On the other, we see the distress and dislocation of societies now entering upon industrialization; we recognize discrepancies between the ideal and the real in our own experience; and we find to our dismay that the Russians—and presumably others as well—are able to build an industrial order upon foundations which challenge many of our most cherished values. As if this were not enough, the technology of mass destruction advances at a pace so swift as to outstrip not simply our control but even our comprehension. Is it conflict and destruction, then, which technology offers us rather than a new freedom? Can hopes prove so unfounded and reality so grim?

I

Despite the contemporary concern such questions represent, they are, after all, far from new. In almost every age men have mingled pride with fear at their own audacity in harnessing nature to serve their ends. In Greek mythology Prometheus—giver of the practical arts of healing and the utilization of the earth's mineral resources, as well as of fire, to mankind—suffered the relentless wrath of Zeus. Christianity, too, consistently has taught men to value material well-being below spiritual, however wide the gap between preachment and practice at any given time. Beyond the limits of western culture, other traditions and philosophies than our own have supported an even more rigorous asceticism. While religious or ideological scruples seem never to have triumphed entirely or for long over countervailing incentives toward earthly comfort and security, strong impulses—rooted no doubt in basic psychological and sociological insights — seem periodically to warn men against the temptation to set too much store by material values, techniques, and achievements. The conflicts, real or presumed, between spiritual and material values which constitute so central a concern of twentieth century thought are contemporary variations, then, on a perennial theme.

From these conflicts we Americans have ourselves by no means been immune. The form they have taken in our experience is, nevertheless, in some respects distinctive. The intellectual foundations of American culture were laid at a period in European history, the seventeenth and eighteenth centuries, when a reconciliation of matter and spirit seemed a reasonable hope in many quarters. Joseph Addison's acknowledgement of a divine "Original" manifest in the material firmament is a familiar expression of this belief. In America a Crevecoeur, Franklin, or Jefferson—even a more sceptical John Adams—would surely have rejected the suggestion that scientific and technical progress were incompatible with human freedom and happiness. Nor have the hopes and expectations of successive generations of immigrants to the United States provided a useful text for sermons on the inevitable conflict between material and spiritual or intellectual concerns. More recently, the unprecedented abundance which Americans in overwhelming numbers enjoy has relieved some at least from the necessity of undue pre-occupation with worldly needs. Taken together, then, it appears that a combination of forces in our history should have alleviated, if not entirely eliminated, the bitterness of traditional controversies.

Yet, to judge by popular interpretations of American culture, one might conclude that these factors have exercised little or no lasting influence on our attitudes and behavior. A few observers to be sure, have discovered in the United States a remarkable freedom from gouging materialism, but their insights have largely been overwhelmed in torrents of social criticism insisting that America somehow uniquely reveals the consequences of a progressive subordination of humane values to technical and materialistic drives.[1] Whatever advantages in origins and circumstances the

---

[1]Among the dissenters, from, and critics of, the prevailing view have been, Jacques Martain, *Reflections on America* (N. Y. 1958) pp. 29-42; David Riesman, *The Lonely Crowd* (Doubleday Anchor Books, 1953), pp. 263-64; also

United States may have enjoyed, it is clear that in the view of many of our most influential and articulate critics we, too, have failed to achieve the hoped-for harmonies. As a symbol and instrument of man's age-old struggles with his material environment, technology seems to have won little more intellectual respectability in America than it has been accorded elsewhere.

While such misgivings have seldom been strong enough to interrupt scientific and technical progress, they have nevertheless greatly distorted appreciation of its social consequences. Despite a record of pragmatic adjustment and social innovation in the face of rapid technical change which can command a modest pride, Americans continue to speak in terms reflecting the preconceptions of an earlier age. At times we behave as if pressing human and social dislocations could be left to find automatic solutions and insist that pre-industrial institutions can encompass the needs of a complex industrial order with little strain and less amendment; at others, faced with the necessity of changes we are unable to accept, we invoke the notion of conspiracy, foreign or domestic, social or intellectual, to justify continued resistance. In such erratic responses the meaning of our actual experience in combining technological change with human advancement eludes recognition. We have claimed too much or too little for the American experiment and, in so doing, have failed to probe the terms of some of our most significant successes and failures.

Events of recent decades indicate that, whatever our ability to pay the price of such confusion and misunderstanding in the past, we can do so no longer. From the depression of the thirties to current and anticipated problems of automation, the rolling impact of industrial technology has made it ever clearer that social stability and well-being under modern conditions must be effortfully won. Revelation of the enormous power of modern techniques of mass communication and of the destructive force of science and technology in a world of clashing nationalisms has aroused new fears and deepened old. On the surface, the record would seem to have confirmed many of the darkest fears of technology's critics. In reality, it demonstrates with undeniable force that rejection of science and technology and neglect of their social implications has become a fatal luxury. The reception accorded so simple a statement of this fact as C. P. Snow's essay, *The Two Cultures and the Scientific Revolution,* reveals widespread discontent with a world

Mary McCarthy, "America The Beautiful," *Commentary,* IV (1947), pp. 201-207, cited by Riesman. See also, David M. Potter, *People of Plenty* (University of Chicago Press, 1954).

in which science and traditional values confront each other across a canyon of prejudice and confusion. Without more imaginative translation into social and humane values, technology bids fare to become the monster its critics have long feared. And without a more meaningful involvement in the material experience of men, the arts deteriorate into private and querulous laments.

II

Nineteenth century American critics of technical progress drew upon a combination of traditional European and uniquely domestic sources for their arguments. The Industrial Revolution, which gave rise in some quarters to extravagant hopes of unlimited social improvement, was less enthusiastically received by those who sensed in it disturbing personal, social, or esthetic implications. Romantic writers fled from factory and town to the countryside, shunning the encroachment of industry and bourgeois values. From Blake's strictures upon England's "dark, satanic mills" to the New England transcendentalists' attitudes toward Boston and the rising industrial order it represented, their reaction was one of deep suspicion, if not outright hostility.[2] Nor was reaction against the impact of industrialization confined to literary circles: its influence can be found in such diverse nineteenth century American movements as the Gothic revival in architecture, early labor and utopian reform programs, nativism, and self-conscious Southern feudalism—each in its way a protest against the rise of an urban, industrial culture.

In Europe, opponents of industrialism could draw support and authority from a landed aristocracy with a tradition of cultural leadership. No such backing was available in democratic America where critics had, therefore, to be more circumspect or more willing to stand alone in their attacks upon a business community increasingly aware of the profits inherent in technological innovation. As business gradually assumed virtual sole patronage over technology, the absence of a self-conscious urban proletariat in the United States meant that opponents of the alliance between technical progress and middle class values lacked still another audience available in Europe. Thus, whether they turned to the upper or to the lower strata of American society, opponents of the advancing industrial technology found a cool reception. While resentment at the speed

---

[2]Leo Marx, "Two Kingdoms of Force: Technology and The Literary Imagination," *The Massachusetts Review,* I (October, 1959), pp. 62-95; Leo Marx, "The Machine in the Garden," *New England Quarterly,* XXIX (March, 1956). pp. 27-42.

and direction of social and technical change could be found at both levels, American "aristocrats" and workers shared too many of the attitudes and ambitions of businessmen, inventors, and artisans to form an effective opposition.[3]

To compensate for the weakness of traditional sources of hostility to middle class materialism and the technological revolution upon which it had seized, America did offer still another social class and, equally important, a social myth whose appeal, while never strong enough to block industrialization, has nevertheless effectively prevented appreciation of its meaning. Ironically, the man whose name and authority have been most effectively invoked by the enemies of industrial technology and its social consequences was Thomas Jefferson. Few more enthusiastic promoters of science and technology can be found in our early history. Yet Jefferson feared the doom of the agrarian society he loved and of democracy itself as a probable outcome of industrialization. His suspicions of the "mobs of large cities" were no less characteristic of the man than was his interest in and support of the work of Eli Whitney. Sufficiently the realist and man of affairs to recognize the irrepressible advance of industrialism, Jefferson late in his career was able to make his own uneasy peace with it; but his commitment to an ideal society of small farmers and independent artisans was fundamentally incompatible with the progress of science and invention to which he was also devoted. This faith in science and technology coupled with a reluctance to face their social consequences are representative of an enduring pattern in American thought. In a kind of double irony, Jefferson's emergence as a full-fledged national hero and symbol of democracy has coincided broadly with the triumph of industrial culture over agrarianism, thus re-emphasizing the ambiguity of American attitudes he so well typifies.

Whatever its author's personal contradictions and hesitations, the tradition of Jeffersonian democracy has proved a strong bulwark against social adaptation to the conditions of industrial life. Jefferson's own resistance to the Federalist program of national economic consolidation; agrarian opposition to tariff subsidies for infant industries; Jacksonian suspicions of an intellectual and scientific elite; Southern resentment of a dynamic, industrial North; Populist and Progressive fears of the implications of large-scale

---

[3]American artists and writers could, and often did, turn to Europe for the social and intellectual support they missed at home. Expatriation was, after all a form of social criticism exemplifying many of the attitudes referred to. The influence of American class structure on social and political thought is discussed with penetration by Louis Hartz, *The Liberal Tradition in America*, (N.Y., 1955).

enterprise; conservative opposition to the new role of government in modern society: each has found in the Jeffersonian tradition strength for resistance to the causes or consequences of technological change. While literary culture has couched its critique of technology primarily in traditional, aristocratic, intellectual terms—themselves the product of a pre-industrial order—Jeffersonian democracy has provided a seedbed for popular confusion as to the nature and needs of a dynamic, technological culture.

Closely allied with the tradition of agrarian democracy is the American faith in the common man, the untutored, unspecialized jack-of-all-trades whose practicality and "know-how" enables him to surpass the achievements of more conventionally privileged contestants in the race for favor and fortune. The practical talents and common sense of the amateur are essentially the hallmark of a relatively undifferentiated, rural way of life, although in a McCormick, Edison, or Ford they marked the transition to industrialization. The American legend of the "self-made" man exercises, thus, a double appeal stemming from roots in our agrarian past as well as relevance to an era of rapid industrialization; but its suitability for a society geared to the dynamisms of science and technology is dubious at best. The sense of anxiety and inadequacy which plagues even the intelligent citizen in this age of specialization and expertise was clearly reflected in President Eisenhower's recent Farewell Address:

> Today, the solitary inventor, tinkering in his shop, has been overshadowed by task forces of scientists in laboratories and testing fields. In the same fashion, the free university, historically the fountainhead of free ideas and scientific discovery, has experienced a revolution in the conduct of research.

> Partly because of the huge cost involved, a Government contract becomes virtually a substitute for intellectual curiosity. For every old blackboard there are now hundreds of new electronic computers.[4]

Outside the economic arena the transition has proved still more difficult for Americans to explain to themselves and accept. The confrontation of agrarian simplicity and virtue with urban-industrial complexity and deviousness has been a perennially popular theme in our literature as well as in our politics. Organized religion in the United States, more than half a century after the rise of the Social Gospel movement, still finds itself desperately struggling to adjust to the facts of industrial life. The temptation for present-day devotees of the comman man to resort to obscurantism

---

[4]New York *Times*, 18 January 1961.

and anti-intellectualism can be documented in popular attitudes toward education and the arts, as well as toward religion, politics, science and technology. For those less actively inclined there remains the ritual release of seeing the experts "stumped" on countless television quiz and panel shows.

Still other examples of the agrarian-industrial confrontation present themselves. While the contemporary cult of the Civil War has drawn its strength from many sources, it is scarcely accidental that this most popular of all episodes in American history is precisely that in which the forces of agrarianism and industrialism faced each other in outright combat. The appeal of the frontier as a refuge from advancing technological society and as a subject for literary and political myth-making rivals that of the Civil War. On the far frontier could be projected perhaps most effectively of all the rugged and simple verities of pre-industrial life.[5]

Americans, thus, have found the agrarian ideal a constant source of inspiration for critiques of industrial society. Yet its attractions have exacted a price in frequent and repeated frustration. Not only have the critics found the industrialists whose ways they deplored appealing to the same symbols and declaring allegiance to identical values; too often the preconceptions and proposals of would-be reformers have also proved monuments to a passing rural order rather than guidelines to a new industrial democracy.[6] Again, no sharper irony can be found, I think, than the sensitivity of contemporary television to the inexhaustible nostalgia of the public it serves. The spectacle of millions of Americans re-living "frontier days" with the aid of all the techniques of modern mass communication is worthy of a Dooley or Mencken. The humorless fury into which the popularity of the TV western drives many of its critics suggests that they resent such bald exposure of the irrelevance to an age of science and technology of the good old days for which they, too, yearn.

III

Indeed, the status and mood of the arts in contemporary America presents an arresting paradox. If ever there were a time in which one might anticipate a new flowering of the creative imagination and a restatement of the perennial themes of human experience in fresh and compelling terms, that time would seem to be the present. Ours is an era of discovery and exploration in which a

---

[5]Henry Nash Smith, *Virgin Land* (Cambridge, 1950), pp. 189-92, 201-6.

[6]Richard Hofstadter *The Age of Reform* (N.Y., 1955), pp. 9-10, 19-20, 242-50, 255-269.

new universe is being exposed to view, full of wonder and hope. Rapid social and economic change presents both strains and opportunities for individuals in many walks of life, as well as new patronage for the arts and the intellect. To this vivid social setting is added the dramatic dimensions of international ideological conflict. Meanwhile, the media through which critical and imaginative insights can reach a broadly literate public are at hand in unparalleled variety. Radio, records, television, magazines, paperbooks, the theatre, libraries, museums, and orchestras, all are patronized as never before in history. The general level of public taste has probably never in history been so high. Americans, young, middle-aged, and elderly alike, have wealth and time at their command to an unprecedented degree. All of these resources, plainly the product of scientific knowledge coupled with technical and organizational ingenuity in its application, lie at our command. Yet the quality of the civilization to which these elements contribute has failed to satisfy either the sensitivity of the artist or the intelligence of the public.

Instead we Americans find ourselves accused of excessive preoccupation with material values. Mass production and the mass market are said to have created a mass taste. Critics may differ as to whether mass culture leads inevitably to the level of the lowest common denominator—"comic book culture"—or whether it merely produces a leveling of taste in which distinctions and gradations of sensitivity are sacrificed to a common standard of mediocrity. In either case they agree that the unique individual vision and its communication are drowned in the insatiable demands of the mass. As in the arts, so in economics, politics, morality, education. Wherever we turn, we are assured that individuality and creative endeavor are being stifled by standardization, commercialism, and apathy. If we are to believe those who fear the encroachments of an impersonal technology, our scientific and technical virtuosity have produced a society in which art is alienated, the individual diminished, intellect trivialized and distracted. No small indictment, indeed!

It is impossible to dismiss as wholly inaccurate or irrelevant either the substance of these charges or the concern they represent. At the same time one suspects that the bemoaners of our technological civilization have failed to comprehend the full range of its qualities and tendencies in their analyses. No simple formula or phrase can adequately describe the revolution in institutions and values through which America has been passing in the course of the last half-century. Its outlines have been sketched and its dimensions suggested but a full appreciation of its character requires the perspectives which only time and more perceptive scrutiny can supply.

Among the fruits of modern technology which, thus far, neither American society nor its critics have successfully savoured or digested is the phenomenon of mass leisure. One hears frequent references to the fact that no other society known to history has made available to its people the resources of time and wealth now at our command, yet the full meaning of this astonishing fact continues to elude us. Statistics showing the reductions which have taken place in the hours and years of labor are sufficiently impressive in themselves, but beyond mere quantitative considerations we can discern the outlines of social revolution. The prospect of mass unemployment and dislocation through automation looms nearer, despite the bravest prophecies of inevitable progress and prosperity. Within the context of work itself a leisure morality has steadily encroached on traditional patterns, as David Riesman and others have noted.[7] Feather-bedding, the coffee break, office parties, and the pleasures of expense-account living raise serious questions not only for the business executive and the tax examiner but for the student of society as well. Together with the growing involvement of both unions and management in the social as well as the working lives of employees, they suggest that the sharpened distinctions between work and leisure which characterized earlier stages of the Industrial Revolution may once again be receding.

Before such fundamental shifts in human relationships, it is scarcely surprising if insight and imagination falter, traditions crumble, and anxiety abounds. To explain the unexpectedly high birth rate which Americans have sustained in recent years, Walt Rostow has suggested that, to avoid the trials and uncertainties of unwonted leisure, we may have chosen to re-impose upon ourselves the disciplines and scarcities that larger families bring.[8] And one is regularly tempted to conclude that we prefer to explore even the relatively certain consequences of mass violence and destruction rather than face the unparalleled possibilities of leisure and plenty now available to us. Forty years ago, it is well to remember, the notion of a ten-hour working day struck many employers as demoralizing and subversive.

The conservatism of vested economic interests in the face of social and political change is a familiar matter. Yet business men

---

[7]David Riesman, *op. cit.,* pp. 305-8.

[8]W. W. Rostow, *The Stages of Economic Growth: a non-Communist Manifesto* (Cambridge University Press, 1960), pp. 11, 80-81.

have managed, with the help of substantial profits, to be sure, to reconcile faith in a progressive technology with adherence to traditional economic values. Our social and intellectual conservatives have been more consistent, if less adaptable. Tracing the threat to established values directly to science and its applications, they have aimed their barbs accordingly. In so doing, they have minimized, when they have not denied, the function of science and technology as fundamental expressions of man's deeply felt need to know and control his environment. Unready for the new conditions of life which material abundance and leisure present, they have heaped scorn—when understanding and imagination were needed—upon society's fumbling efforts to incorporate these riches into new patterns and opportunities.

IV

Responsibility for the reaction against science and technology can be charged only in part to conservatism and bias on the part of vested cultural interests. Equal contributors have been the over-enthusiastic spokesmen for science and material progress themselves. Sharing the widespread utopianism which science helped to sustain, these men—much like the abolitionists, pacifists, and other reformers of the nineteenth century—tended to believe that their new techniques alone held the key to the fulfillment of all human needs and the reconstruction of society. As the prestige of science and engineering soared with successive achievements, extravagant optimism and a casual dismissal of disturbing social implications were readily encouraged.[9] These heightened the sense of displacement and alienation among the devotees of the ancient culture, steeped as they were in a more sensitive evaluation of human ambiguities and a less obviously materialistic ideal of social harmony. Out of injured pride on the one hand and smug complacency on the other grew the resentments which divided the intellectual community into opposing camps.

Yet by the beginning of the twentieth century, science itself was moving in a direction which eventually made possible a reunification of divergent values and points of view. The history of science and technology in America, as elsewhere, shows a steady progression toward professionalism and specialization out of the amateur status they so often enjoyed in the early phases of the Industrial Revolution. The gentleman-scientist and the artisan-inventor, familiar figures well into the nineteenth century, are

---

[9]Rene Dubos, *The Dreams of Reason* (N.Y., 1961), pp. 101, 149-52.

familiar no longer. The career of Thomas Edison illustrates the rapidity with which sepecialization overtook one of this country's legendary scientist-inventors. Matthew Josephson shows that, while Edison in the 1870's was able without benefit of formal training to carry on significant experimentation at the forefront of knowledge in the field of electricity, by 1900 he had been left far behind through the development of organized industrial research and professional scientific and technical education.[10] Paralleling the advance of specialization has been the liberation of science and technology from domination by "practical" and material interests alone and their emergence as pre-eminently intellectual disciplines. The rapid narrowing of the gap between application and theory in science has led to new appreciation of the role of ideas and imagination as its truly creative elements. James B. Conant has compared the theoretical structures of modern science with the Parthenon and the medieval cathedrals as monuments of the human spirit; no one today would seriously deny the claims of science to an honored place in the record of man's intellectual achievements.[11]

Similarly, the traditional contempt of the down-to-earth engineer for the theoretician, a standard theme of nineteenth century discussions, is rapidly passing away. In an urban-industrial context, furthermore, advances in technology impinge upon social conditions with an often startling immediacy. As the engineer comes to recognize that the success of his efforts depends frequently as much upon human factors as upon technical, the practical basis for co-operation and understanding between humanist and technician is rapidly being extended. As the nineteenth century brought growing recognition of the mutual dependence of science and technology, so it now appears the twentieth promises a further re-unification of these disciplines with the social sciences and the arts.

The very fruitfulness of modern conceptual science has produced a deeper sense of the limits, as well as the extraordinary power, of this system of thought. The scientist has come face to face with the fundamental fact of his inability, however sophisticated his techniques, to escape the confines of his own perceptual apparatus; and this, in turn, has led to a new caution and humility in advancing the claims of reason alone to comprehend the universe and disclose its universally applicable laws.[12] Science has increasingly recognized the extent to which it shares with other forms

---

[10]Matthew Josephson, *Edison, a Biography* (N.Y., 1959) pp. 411-13, 466-67

[11]James B. Conant, *Modern Science and Modern Man,* (Doubleday Anchor Books, 1952), pp. 99, 187.

[12]*Ibid.,* pp. 55-101; Dubos, *op. cit.,* pp. 102-2.

of thought in the tentative character of all human experience and achievement. Meanwhile, the raw destructiveness of uncontrolled science arouses men of all talents to explore more diligently the terms of their common humanity. In the search for a more humane world, science, technology, and the arts share a joint dependence and responsibility.

V

Recognizing in technology and related disciplines a dimension of man's experience no less valid than others can free us, at last, from past controversies to face the insistent issues of today. A realistic analysis can no longer dismiss the vulgarity, futility, and cruelty which characterize so much of contemporary culture merely by attributing them to an essentially brute technology. Much more study is needed of the conditions which foster or hamper the creative release of human and material resources. Even more than new facts, however, we need the stimulus which only new conceptions of the structure and ends of a dynamic, technological civilization can supply. Past experience indicates all too clearly the frustrations which result either from blind acceptance or blind rejection of technological change; and both acceptance and rejection will remain essentially blind until a new framework of social understanding enlarges our vision.

The issue is not merely of academic, but of practical and immediate, concern. Daily decisions as well as long-range programs inevitably hinge upon social and individual priorities arising from concepts, however vague, of an ideal social order. Whether we choose better schools or lower taxes, billboards or beauty on our highways, respectability or misery for our aged, definition of problems and choice of measures appropriate to them will reflect a system of valued means and ends. When this system is not subjected to critical re-examination, particularly at times of rapid social change, it inevitably distorts the policies through which we attempt to manage our lives. The problem which science and technology pose for contemporary society lies precisely here, that they make re-evaluation of ends and means at once more necessary and more difficult.

Nor it is enough to label the resulting impasse as an example of "cultural lag" and let it go at that. While the concept may help us to define the problem, it has proved less useful than once was hoped in enabling us to surmount our difficulties.[13] Too often it has

---

[12]See William F. Ogborn, *Social Change* (Viking Press, 1950 edition), p. 200.

served to enable us to deplore society's plight while minimizing its capacity for remedial action. Science and technology have made possible, for Americans and for an as yet undetermined portion of the rest of mankind, a "new world." We Americans have taken pride in our contributions to technical progress, to the point at times of exaggerating them. It is equally true, I believe, that our social institutions have demonstrated a remarkable capacity to absorb and adapt to change. The modern business corporation, the community chest, the American system of education, and the Tennessee Valley Authority—to cite several familiar examples—testify to an impressive degree of social ingenuity. Such social inventiveness, however, has won less recognition than it deserves; and it is still fashionable to deplore helplessly an essentially mythical contrast between progressive technology and a supposedly changeless social order.

One reason for our failure to take full credit for a record of social adaptation which the experience of other nations has shown to be commendable lies, surely, in a realistic sense of imperfect achievement. A second source of our excessive modesty can be found, I believe, in the lingering appeal of pre-industrial values and traditions. The advocates and architects of social change in the United States have usually felt constrained to justify their handiwork not in functional terms, primarily, but in the language of an earlier day. The conservatism of American social philosophy has thus obscured American daring in social experimentation. We continue to preach "individual enterprise" as we practice highly centralized private and public planning. In government we still defer to "states' rights" a century after the Civil War, while evolving an intricate, if not very efficient, system of national controls and initiative. In education we struggle manfully, although not always successfully, to balance general education for effective citizenship with the insistent demand for specialized knowledge. That we have managed in the face of entrenched resistance to achieve any social advances at all is a tribute both to the strength of the forces which impel us to search out new directions and to our ingenuity, or luck, in shooting the rapids of social change while pretending to lie at anchor.

It is in the light of this experience that the new mass leisure and the media which serve it can be more effectively studied. As fruits of a new technology offering choices and resources never before so widely accessible, their use can be guided and enlivened by traditional values, to be sure; but new insights and imaginative departures from established patterns will be equally necessary. That these new resources have contributed to a strong and active popular interest in the arts is already clear. Similarly, one has only to travel the country to confirm the fact that long-standing differences between rural and urban life are being drastically modified. Farming has become a major industry in the do-it-yourself suburbs; urban renewal promises parks and green belts in the metropolis; factories and their workers invade and obliterate the fields. At the same time, by land, sea, and air, Americans in unprecedented numbers sample the landscapes and experiences which a continent, a planet, and, indeed, a solar system offer. That the consequences of this social explosion are often offensive to the senses and the intellect is undeniable. To persist in judging them by pre-industrial standards is both unilluminating and futile.

As contemporary American culture is approached, not with the hauteur of old habits but in a spirit which searches for new patterns and potentialities, both our understanding and our capacity for self-direction may be greatly enhanced. There is no reason to imagine, certainly at this early date, that a simple formula or standard will emerge to guide us in achieving a harmonious balance between freedom and control, spontaneity and discipline, chaos and over-organization in modern life. It may well be that differing times and circumstances warrant a sensitive and continuous adjustment of our social scales. New levels of knowledge and material wealth make possible, if they do not necessarily foster, more sophisticated social controls than we have relied on in the past. Nor need answers be sought always through the application of more sweeping political controls. The mess which private initiative has created in television may well call for experimentation with new forms of public competition and control in the interest of taste and variety. Yet, in another sector, it now seems probable that relaxation of public and private policies governing the ages of employment and retirement will prove desirable. The simple truth is that it is not technology but our own inertia and lack of imagination which have produced the cultural excesses we deplore.

To trace in detail the record of American responses to technological change or to offer specific prescriptions for the social ills accompanying the impact of modern science would be inappropriate here. Rather, I have tried to indicate what I believe to be a paradox at the core of American culture. Despite our technological virtuosity and our commitment as a people to a broad sharing of the benefits it makes possible, we have achieved no consensus as to the quality and character of the industrial civilization we want. Whatever our shortcomings in institutional adaptation to change, a more fundamental weakness can be found in our failure to envision in compelling terms the framework and ends of a democratic society in full mastery of the dynamic forces of science and technology. Institutions ultimately function no better than the human understanding which informs and shapes them. Without more adequate conceptions of what technology offers, and upon what terms, our adaptations are piecemeal and ramshackle at best.

Such conceptions can emerge only from a union of intellect and imagination in common concern for the quality of social and individual life; all the resources of the arts and sciences can now be joined in such an undertaking. Upon our ability to achieve a greater harmony among these discordant elements of American culture, indeed, depends the ultimate meaning of technology for our time.

PUBLIC OPINION—A DEMOCRATIC DILEMMA

By STOW PERSONS

Stow Persons is Professor of History at the State University of Iowa. He is the author of an outstanding textbook in American intellectual history entitled AMERICAN MINDS. He is the editor of a new publication entitled SOCIAL DARWINISM: SELECTED ESSAYS of WILLIAM GRAHAM SUMNER. He is currently editing Laurence Gronlund's COOPERATIVE COMMONWEALTH.

Almost from the very beginnings of colonial settlement in Anglo-America, more than three centuries ago, governments have taken the form that would be classified, broadly speaking, as the popular type. Even the Puritans formally affirmed the theory of popular sovereignty, though their practice seems to us to have been a caricature of that principle. The whole course of American political development might be characterized, not improperly, as a quest for more effective popular government.

I

While the implementation of the theory of popular government may be accomplished in a variety of ways, at least one constant factor will always be present. This is the responsiveness of public officials to the will of the people, expressed in the form to which we have attached the term, public opinion. For us, public opinion is simply the articulation of that sovereign authority that embodies the ultimate will of the community. Every political thinker and every reflective politician from the days of John Winthrop to those of Franklin Roosevelt would have assented to these propositions.

One might appropriately assume, therefore, that American political theorists, working as they all have within the traditions of popular government, would have had a good deal to say about so fundamental an aspect of political life as the characteristics of public opinion. In fact, however, this is not at all the case. Conditioned as we have become in recent times to an intense—almost morbid—preoccupation with public opinion and its dictates, it is doubly surprising to discover that until very recent years American political theorists have had virtually nothing to say on this subject. The general histories of American political thought ignore the matter. With the sole exception of some fragmentary investigations by Professor Francis Wilson I have been unable to find any indication that historians have concerned themselves with the subject.[1] The reason for this neglect is found, of course, in the fact that the sources the historian uses, namely, the writings of political theorists, do not deal explicitly with public opinion save for an occasional parenthetical remark. Not until the early years of the twentieth century did analysis of public opinion take its place among the fundamental problems of democratic political theory.

The temptation to speculate on the causes of so remarkable an oversight is almost overwhelming. Why was it that the political thinkers of the eighteenth and nineteenth centuries could have ignored so fundamental and obvious a branch of their subject? Walter Lippman asked this same question forty years ago, and he suggested an ingenious explanation.[2] Every living political faith, said Mr. Lippmann, contains a central axiom or assumption upon which the whole system rests. The validity of the axiom itself is taken for granted, not simply for the logical reason that any system of thought must rest on some premises, but also for the practical reason that men are less likely to challenge assumptions of which they are unaware. In the democratic ideology the central unexamined axiom is the sovereignty of public opinion, and for many years this axiom remained hidden from view in the innermost sanctuary of the public piety.

However esthetically satisfying Mr. Lippmann's disposition of this problem may be, it does not absolve the historian from the prosaic task of conducting his own investigation. After all, Mr. Lippmann wrote as a political philosopher and not as a historian, and as every hard-working historian knows, no temptation is stronger than the temptation to substitute a theory for research. But the difference between the philosopher and the historian is scarcely indicated by the mere fact that the philosopher passes up the opportunity to play tricks on the dead. The philosopher quite properly looks at his problems from his own point of view. He

---

[1]Francis G. Wilson, "The Federalist on Public Opinion," *Public Opinion Quarterly*, IV (1940), pp. 563-575; "James Bryce on Public Opinion: Fifty Years Later," *Ibid.*, III (1939), pp. 420-435.

[2]*Public Opinion* (New York, 1922), 254-255.

stands at the center of his universe, and his own mind is the focal point on which all experience is centered. For this very reason, I think, a good philosopher is likely to be a bad historian because the historian must purge himself of the natural and healthy human impulse to place himself or his times at the center of the human drama, and to interpret his own advent as its fitting and proper climax. So far as he is a good historian he will attempt to detach himself imaginatively from the conventions and assumptions of his own day and age in order to minimize that form of distortion which flows from the common tendency to explain the past in terms of the present.

Applied to our present problem, such reflections may serve as a caveat to look again at the question as it was first phrased. On further scrutiny it is obvious that to ask why something did not happen in history—or at least why it did not happen sooner—is a singularly inept question, the sooner abandoned the better. It should also be apparent that our first impulse to search for the reasons why the theory of public opinion had for so long been ignored reflected the implicit assumption that the modern preoccupation with public opinion is a proper and inevitable concern, and that it is therefore necessary to discover why our forebears had been so benighted as to overlook it. This temporal provincialism is, of course, precisely the kind of fallacy against which I have suggested that it is a prime function of the historical style of thinking to guard. By what right do we assume that wisdom and virtue are on our side, and that history may properly be summoned to the bar of this day and age? As a salutary corrective, let us experiment with turning the question around, and instead of inquiring why Americans succeeded in evading the theory of public opinion for so long, ask rather how it came about that in spite of the practical experience and accumulated wisdom of more than two centuries of popular government, Americans in our own times could yet be seduced by the blandishments of utopians or demagogues into subscribing to the preposterous notion that a stable foundation for political society could be found in the direct expressions of public opinion? Needless to say, I do not offer this question as an adequate working hypothesis. But I do suggest that it is no more arbitrary than the commonly received alternative.

In brief then, the object of this review will be to inquire into the train of events and ideas that led to the modern theory of public opinion. And we will try to maintain the pose that the modern state of affairs was not a foreordained outcome, not the inevitable product of a matured political intelligence, but that a succession of circumstances, each with its own contingencies, led to this particular outcome rather than to some other.

II

If we commence our survey more or less arbitrarily with the eighteenth century era of independence and constitution making, we must strive to do justice to the peculiar American relationship between theory and practice. Americans had deeply rooted traditions of colonial self-government, and their political philosophy could and frequently did skim lightly over topics upon which the judgements of experience appeared to be firmly fixed. For our present purposes, one of these topics was the nature and functions of representation. And representative institutions are the key to the whole problem.

The theory and functions of representation were not extensively discussed in eighteenth century writings, perhaps for the very reason that a distinctive pattern was well developed in all of the colonies before the Revolution.[3] Everywhere, the popularly elected legislative assemblies provided the circumstances within which this pattern was nourished. Save in two small colonies, Connecticut and Rhode Island, the colonial legislators were the most important and sometimes the only public officials to be chosen by the electors. The requirements or qualifications which surrounded their selection were of great significance. First, a residence requirement, both for suffrage and for candidacy for office was usual, though not universal. Annual terms of office were also usual. Everywhere, the intimacy of association of office seeker with the electorate was a striking feature. Electoral districts were numerically small, usually numbering their votes in the mere hundreds. The absence of political parties meant that campaigns for office had to be conducted by the candidates themselves, who had to be personally known to the voters to have much chance of success. The weight of these factors was so great that the theorist could take it for granted that in America the representative represented his constituents and no one else, regardless of what the contemporaneous British theory of virtual representation might hold. Furthermore, although the Massachusetts practice of instruction by the constituency was exceptional, the American representative tended to be something of a delegate, scrupulously regardful of the views of

---

[3] For a perceptive discussion of the development of the theory and practices of representation in America see Alfred de Grazia, *Public and Republic: Political Representation in America* (New York, 1951).

the majority of his constituents, especially if he wished to remain in office. These practices might be characterized as direct constituency representation, a form of representation which has always remained a principal feature of the American political system.

It is true that during the later eighteenth century an alternative theory of interest representation was popular with conservative theorists and constitution makers. According to this theory, advocated most notably by James Madison and John Adams, means should be devised to secure representation of the different interests in the community. In practice, this boiled down to finding ways in which to protect the rich from the poor. It is instructive to observe that even at that early date the rich were on the defensive, and were hence compelled to master the gentle arts of recouping in the market place the losses suffered at the polling place. Although historians have frequently referred to Madison's exposition of the theory of interest representation in *Federalist* # 10, it seems to me that the significance of the theory has been rather overestimated. In spite of the common recourse to the bicameral legislature with differing property qualifications both for membership and electorate, interest representation found hard sledding in the states, where it survived for scarcely more than a generation.

The prevailing characteristics of direct constituency representation were confirmed and strengthened by the Federal character of American government under the Constitution of 1787, and by the rise of political democracy in the early nineteenth century. Because the Constitution provided for a federal union of sovereign states, it was inevitable that Senators as well as Congressmen should represent their respective States, regardless of the expectations of Alexander Hamilton, who hoped that Senators at least would emancipate themselves from parochial interests.

The impact of democracy upon representation was perhaps even more decisive. Short terms and rotation in office, the conversion of appointive to elective offices, proposals to abolish the Electoral College and to make United States Senators and State governors popularly elective, all reflected the democratic impulse to make representative institutions responsive to the public will as expressed by the majority. The rise of democratic political parties also served to strengthen and implement constituency representation. From the beginning, these parties were federations of state parties rather than centralized national parties. Their electoral techniques were sensitively attuned to the impulses which were expressing themselves in direct representation. As constituencies became larger, and the electoral process necessarily more impersonal, it became the prime function of the party to reduce political ideas and problems to manageable proportions. This was accomplished by simplifying issues to alternative patterns between which voters could choose, and particularly by identifying issues with personalities, the candidates for office. My point here is that the rise of the political party is to be understood not as the intervention of a third force between the constituent and the office holder, but, at least in part, as the fashioning of a device suitable to modern conditions for mediating between voter and representative.[4]

This kind of direct constituency representation achieved its appropriate fulfillment in the reduction of the function of a representative to that of an agent. In the words of the journalist, Parke Godwin, "A representative is but the mouthpiece and organ of his constituents. What we want in legislation as in other trusts, are honest fiduciaries, men who will perform their duties according to our wishes."[5] It was appropriate, therefore, for Godwin and those who thought like him, to sanction the practice of instructing representatives. Several state constitutions made such provision, apart from the informal practice of state legislatures in instructing U. S. Senators whom they had chosen. The rationale behind the practice of instruction was stated categorically by the journalist Hezekiah Niles, in 1825; "The people are generally right, and, at any rate, their opinions are the only opinions that can be safely respected as reaching that degree of infallibility which is presumed to exist in every government . . . ."[6] The Virginia legislature had declared that laws reflected the general will, and that "the general will is only the result of individual wills fairly collected and compared."[7] Hence the appropriateness of furnishing explicit instructions.

I have stressed the theory and practice of constituency representation because out of it was precipitated the modern preoccupation with public opinion as a political problem. During much of the nineteenth century the concept of public opinion seems to have occupied the same kind of position with respect to popular sovereignty as did suffrage. Popular sovereignty was admittedly meaningless without an informed and responsible public

---

[4] A succinct acknowledgement of the proper responsiveness of a democratic political party to its constituency was contained in a manifesto of fourteen Pennsylvania Congressmen issued in 1824. See *Niles Weekly Register,* XXV (Jan. 27, 1824), pp. 306-307.

[5] *Political Essays* (1856), quoted in de Grazia, p. 124.

[6] *Niles Weekly Register,* XXVIII (May 28, 1825), p. 193.

[7] de Graiza, p. 126.

opinion, and unless men could implement that opinion effectively through the use of the franchise. And yet the striking historical fact is that these associations were not frequently and explicitly made. Every thoughtful student of history knows how the logic of a situation runs ahead of practical behavior. In this case, the institutions of representation stood between government and the popular will. Any potential concern for the theory of public opinion was submerged within the preoccupation with direct representation.

A theory was nevertheless present, even though in embryo, and those who were disturbed by its implications were quicker to explore its meaning than were those who complacently took it for granted. James Madison stated the theory succinctly when he observed that public opinion was the opinion of the majority; and he expressed his own reservations about it when he added that it would always reflect the interests of the majority.[8] Again, John C. Calhoun was at pains to show that the assumptions of the prevailing practice of direct constituency representation rested on a theory of public opinion which was inadequate because it provided no solution to the problem of protecting the rights of the minority.[9]

The assumptions of constituency representation had become so firmly rooted in the American political consciousness that when, by the end of the nineteenth century, representative institutions began to sag under the impact of industrial concentration, urbanization, and utilities monopolies, the obvious solution seemed to be to secure the same object, namely, implementation of the will of the majority, more effectively by resort to expressions of that will through forms of direct democracy. Alfred de Grazia has pointed out how the social and political problems of the 'nineties were understood by populists, reformers, debtors, and progressives in terms of their conditioning in the representative tradition.[10] They found good government being balked by malevolent individuals, such as monopolists and speculators, working through bosses and corrupt political machines. The solution they proposed was to circumvent institutions no longer truly representative by having recourse to such forms of direct democracy as the initiative, referendum, recall of officers and of judicial decisions, ballot reform, and women suffrage. All of these were devices calculated to imple-

---

[8] Madison, *Letters and Other Writings* (4 vols. Philadelphia, 1867), I, p. 326.

[9] Calhoun, "Disquisition on Government," *Works* (Cralle ed.), I, pp. 1-39.

[10] de Grazia, 178.

ment effective majority rule. They admittedly presupposed a higher standard of citizenship, in terms of which ignorance and apathy were now to be branded major political sins. Political maturity and public spirit were now to be equated with active political participation. And in all of this there was considerable confusion of political techniques with programmatic objectives.

The utopian strain in the thinking of the direct democrats was clearly apparent in Frank Parsons, one of the most active and vocal of the proponents of direct legislation. Successively civil engineer, lawyer, law professor, and reformer, Parsons gave himself over wholly to the cause of progressive reform at the urban and state levels. Direct democracy, he believed, would purify political life by drawing better men into politics, by minimizing partisanship, purifying the press, and educating the public. Direct democracy would somehow restore a proper political balance between the rich and the poor. But at the same time, the intelligent and public spirited citizens who would take the trouble to study issues and vote in referenda as the occasion offered would gain an advantage over the uninformed and uninterested citizens too preoccupied with their private affairs to exert themselves politically. Parsons evaded the unpalatable ideological implications of this distinction by persuading himself that in a democratic society in which civic responsibility was taught to be an obligation it could safely be assumed that the public spirited citizens would constitute a majority. Majority opinion, therefore, could safely be accepted as both morally and politically superior to minority opinion. Like many other Progressives, Parsons was concerned chiefly with the formulation of public policy, to which end he conceived the techniques of direct democracy to be appropriate means, and he gave little thought to the rights of the minority or to their protection.[11]

What was significant in this line of thinking was that it led directly to the unmasking of public opinion. The assumptions involved in the thinking of the direct democrats continued to be the assumptions of many of those concerned with public opinion as an aspect of the political process. Thus, for instance, George Gallup tells us that the function of the pollster is to ascertain public opinion more precisely than can the politician using traditional techniques of sounding his constituency.[12]

[11]Parsons, *Direct Legislation* (Equity Series II, no. 2; Philadelphia, 1900) pp. 6-30.

[12]Gallup, *Public Opinion in a Democracy* (Stafford Little Lecture, Princeton University, 1939).

But when did public opinion emerge from the chrysalis of representation to pursue a career under its own colors? Without attempting to fix a precise date, I think we can risk the guess that it was somewhere around 1890. Professor Wilson says that Bryce, whose *American Commonwealth* was published in 1888, was one of the most important of the writers who made the modern world conscious of the problems of public opinion.[13] And yet, in spite of all that Bryce had to say about the influence of opinion in America, he still found its expression in the institutions of political representation.

Here is a paragraph from the St. Louis *Globe-Democrat,* in 1893, which will serve to signalize the arrival of public opinion in its own right, independent of all forms of implementation:

> It is trite to say that public opinion is the supreme power in this country; but the fact is illustrated now and then in a way which gives it special interest and significance. Nobody can tell just how the force is generated, or just how it makes itself decisively felt in given emergencies. When we undertake to trace it to its origin and analyze its development, we are soon lost in a bewilderment of surmise and conjecture, from which nothing definite can be derived. There are times, we know, when a certain opinion or sentiment begins to make its way over the country, apparently from many different strating points, and it grows day by day until finally it becomes predominant, gaining recognition in legislation and substituting one policy for another in the regulation of our affairs. The people in various localities seem somehow to think the same thoughts upon a subject at the same time, without collusion or any chance of consultation, and the first thing we know the influence thus set in motion is directing the course of events in spite of all opposition. It is a great psychological mystery which our statesmen and philosophers have not yet been able to solve.[14]

It was indeed a great mystery, and we can begin to appreciate the good sense or good fortune of earlier students of public affairs who were content to assume that the techniques of direct constituency representation gave effective voice to public opinion, and to refrain either deliberately or instinctively from probing the mystery directly.

There is no doubt a universal impulse of human nature to bend the ear at times to a delphic utterance that is accepted as the voice of God, no matter what gibberish it may pronounce. But at least a few thoughtful Americans had a firm enough grasp upon the democratic ideal as a normative concept to insist that qualitative

---

[13]*Public Opinion Quarterly,* III (1939), p. 420.

[14]Quoted in *Public Opinion,* XV (Sept. 23, 1893), p. 575.

126

considerations should not be lost from sight. The *Baltimore Sun* declared in 1889 that public opinion was not a consensus of the opinions of everyone; if it were, it would be merely a compromise, inferior to the best opinion. The *Sun* was prepared to believe that in fact public opinion was usually the opinion of the wisest leaders, due to the fact that the strongest men furnished the unthinking masses with their opinions. But by the same token, public opinion should always be challenged by thoughtful citizens whenever they believed it to be misguided, for then it might be set right. The *Sun* was inclined to view public opinion as the outcome of a Social Darwinian struggle for the control of men's minds. "Public opinion follows the leaders who triumph in a battle of reason."[15] This ingenious effort to salvage quality from numbers, to get an *ought* from an *is,* must command our admiration, even if it leaves us unconvinced.

IV

No sooner had public opinion been isolated as an ingredient of public affairs, than it was subjected to searching criticism from two different quarters. On the one hand, the new social science of sociology insisted upon viewing the problem from a broader and more detached perspective. Professor William Graham Sumner of Yale made a characteristic distinction between the basic psychological matrix within which social life is embedded and public opinion defined as attitudes towards public affairs. The former was composed of the inherited patterns of behavior and belief, the mores and folkways, that governed men's conduct. This psychological matrix was subject to very gradual change in response to basic technological and economic changes. It might perhaps be regarded as public opinion of a kind; but in comparison with it, public opinion in the ordinary sense of the term—that is, attitudes towards public affairs—was of only trivial importance as an element in the social process.[16]

Lester F. Ward took a similar position when he distinguished between the *Zeitgeist,* "that part of human thought which lies below all doubt, question, schism, or discussion," and public opinion. The latter consisted of the questions under discussion, the issues that divided men. Questions closed to discussion, such as democracy, monogamy, or the separation of church and state, were part of the *Zeitgeist* of our society.[17]

---

[15]Quoted in *Public Opinion,* VIII (Nov. 23, 1889), pp. 168-169.

[16]Summer, *Folkways* (Boston and New York, 1906), pp. 2-4, 16-20, 30-59.

[17]Ward, *Applied Sociology* (Boston and New York, 1906), p. 44.

The sociological distinction between the fundamental unifying forces in the community and the relatively superficial attributes of public opinion permitted the Michigan sociologist Charles Horton Cooley to state the problem in a different way. Approaching public opinion as an aspect of the social process, Cooley defined it as a "certain ripeness and stability of thought resulting from attention and discussion." It was not to be understood necessarily as agreement or disagreement upon some question of policy. Admittedly, a body of agreed opinion was the usual definition because of the common presumption that public opinion was the basis for decision and action. But Cooley insisted that while decision and action might result, they were not of the essence of the definition. After all, the resultant action might be a compromise, or there might be no action at all; yet the formation of a public opinion on the matter might be of great importance. Public opinion, then, was deliberation rather than agreement. The superficial conception of public opinion as agreement was considered by Cooley to be a remnant of the eighteenth-century idea that men are normally isolated and that social life consists of their coming together or agreeing in certain ways. Such a view failed to do justice to minorities, conceiving of them as stubborn refractory remnants.

Public opinion properly conceived was part of the social process, a complex growth forming and dissolving in time and perhaps partially unified on occasion for action. So far as people displayed sufficient interest in affairs to discuss them, there was public opinion, even though no common conclusions emerged. "Communicated differences are the life of opinion, as cross-breeding is of a natural stock." From a dynamic point of view, Cooley believed that great importance attached to the role of the minority. All notable change began in the comprehension of a few only. Originality, faith, desire for improvement were always found in the minority, while every majority was composed of inert and dependent elements. Therefore, Cooley concluded, if one wished to consult public opinion as a means of prognosis, let him look to the minority, not because the minority must necessarily become a working majority, but because creative leadership was to be found there. "There is nothing more democratic than intelligent and devoted non-conformity, because it means that the individual is giving his freedom and courage to the service of the whole. Subservience, to majorities as to any other authority, tends to make vigorous democracy impossible."[18] These were noble sentiments

[18]Cooley, *The Social Process* (1909. New York ed., 1927) pp. 378-381.

to which we all breathe a fervent Amen, but where did they leave public opinion?

V

A second line of attack was taken by traditionalists who argued that representative institutions provided a more valid and defensible expression of public opinion than did the techniques of direct democracy. In 1907, the elder Senator Henry Cabot Lodge readily acknowledged the dependence of representation upon public opinion. It was precisely the public forum for responsible debate provided by the legislative chamber that, in Lodge's eyes, furnished the necessary link between public opinion and public policy. In contrast the devices of direct democracy made no provision for discussion. In the referendum, the voter would be presented with a ballot upon which he was to express a preference with or without benefit of discussion of the issues, as the circumstances of the individual voter might determine. Lodge thus attempted to turn the weapon of public opinion upon opponents who must have thought themselves in firm possession of it.[19]

Much the most extended and discriminating discussion of the problems of public opinion within the context of traditional political assumptions was furnished by Abbot Lawrence Lowell of Harvard in his *Public Opinion and Popular Government* (1913). Lowell took up the question where the sociologists had left it. His problem was to mediate between the universally accepted mores or *Zeitgeist* and the controversial issues of opinion. His solution leaned markedly toward the former alternative. He was prepared to define an opinion as a public opinion when its implementation was acceptable to the minority in spite of its opposition. Thus the issue must clearly fall within the ends of policy and methods of government upon which the whole community was agreed. This was a profoundly conservative view. Lowell was at pains to emphasize the great restraints under which a government responsive to public opinion as truly conceived must operate. Public Opinion as he understood it functioned in much the same way as did Calhoun's notorious concurrent majority.

The events of the First World War introduced radically new elements and thus transformed the terms of the discussion. The war of 1917 was the first ideological war in American history. For the first time, a deliberate manipulation of mass opinion by

---

[19]Lodge, *The Democracy of the Constitution and Other Essays and Addresses* (New York, 1915), pp. 1-31.

governmental agencies was undertaken. The propaganda campaign rested on the assumption that the maximum war effort could be obtained only by persuading the American people that theirs was the cause of civilization and righteousness, and that the enemy represented tyranny, deceit, and inhumanity. Unquestionably, the campaign was oversold. The cynicism of the 'twenties was just one facet of the deeper sophistication which flowered from the painful realization of a gullible and innocent people that they had been used. Public opinion as a subject of study became indissolubly wed to propaganda, a union which is witnessed in virtually every textbook even today. The effect of these circumstances was clearly apparent in the writing of Walter Lippmann in the early 'twenties. Before the War, the central issues had been concerned with the nature and implementation of public opinion, with the ways in which public opinion was suitably translated into public policy. Now, however, in the second phase of the discussion, it was apparent to Mr. Lippmann that the assumption earlier taken for granted, namely, that the average citizen is both capable and willing to form adequate opinions about the world around him, must itself be subjected to careful scrutiny. What had been done deliberately in wartime appeared to be merely a special case of the distortion that always entered into the formation of opinions about the external world. Man's normal behavior was governed by symbolic pictures or stereotypes compounded of the individual's sense of values and his observations of life. These stereotypes varied enormously in adequacy, but were always simpler and more rigid than the flux of events.

Public opinion, Lippmann believed, was inevitably conditioned by the circumstances of group life. The stereotypes governing individual behavior were shaped largely by the community. In the formation of public opinions, individually centered emotions were transferred by means of conditioned responses to certain public symbols, to which were attached the desired policies. Lippmann clearly understood the emotional involvement which transformed a passive idea into a politically potent public opinion. The real opinion makers were the individual's associates, his parents, friends, teachers, employers, and colleagues. The forces at work in the process were those that in part assured the unity and solidarity of the community.

It was no longer possible, therefore, to accept the traditional assumption of democratic theory that political society was composed of self-sufficient individuals. The conversion of private opinions formed in the manner just indicated into public opinions required the subordination of the personal factors ordinarily involved in opinion formation to the objectivity and patience necessary to the fashioning of adequate opinions about the external world.

Lippmann concluded that only after a thorough education, after the attainment of adequate economic resources, with the possession of leisure, and with accurate information available could individuals hope to form opinions that would meet the qualitative criteria of public opinion. It was no longer possible to be as complacent on this matter as the pre-war generation had been.

VI

The third and final phase of the discussion of public opinion is concerned with efforts to measure public opinion quantitatively. Heretofore, theorists had been preoccupied with the place of public opinion in political theory. So far as I am capable of judging, nothing more of significance has been said on that subject since the 'twenties. In other respects, however, popular interest in the matter had then scarcely commenced. George Gallup organized the American Institute of Public Opinion in 1935, and that date may be taken as the conventional starting point of the current practice of public opinion surveys.

But the pollster is interested in private opinions rather than in public opinion as traditionally conceived. He has devised elaborate techniques for the development of questionnaires free from distortion or ambiguity. He has mastered the statistical problems of sampling, and he has perfected the organization that makes national and even international surveys of opinion possible. With these aspects of opinion measurement I have no quarrel, nor indeed have I the competence to discuss them critically. The question which I raise is simply the question whether the individual opinions that the pollster records in answer to his inquiry constitute public opinion. The validity of the sample is not in question. But the political reality of the thing sampled is.

It seems to me that the pollster, by eliciting casual responses to his own arbitrarily chosen questions, is actually creating a partially artificial opinion which he labels "public opinion." Furthermore, he appears to be largely oblivious of the profound consequences of this irresponsible act of creation. The pressures for conformity about which we hear so much nowadays are the result in part of a deliberately cultivated sensitivity to whatever is alleged to be public opinion.

It is no accident, I suspect, that public opinion polling and its rationale are products of the academic mind rather than of the practical political world. The opinion survey fails to make a distinction, crucial for political purposes, between what might be called active and passive opinions. Active opinions are those held with such conviction or felt to be of such practical importance to those who hold them as to impel these individuals to seek their actual implementation. As we say, they make their opinions felt as well as known. Passive opinions, on the other hand, are those which all of us hold on many subjects, and which we willingly indicate to the pollster when he questions us, but in which we are not sufficiently involved to work actively for their realization. As a practical matter, the politician will necessarily be concerned primarily with the active opinions of his constituents. Successful politicians working within representative institutions have always recognized this distinction. Democratic theory would probably prefer not to have to grapple with the distinction between active and passive opinions, but this is a dilemma which the unmasking of public opinion forces upon it.

But I cannot gainsay the fact that while polling may neglect some of the implicit assumptions of constituency representation, it does appear to be in accord with the theory of direct democracy. In this respect, polling is the authentic culmination of a clearly marked development. Just as John Adams felt no dishonor in receiving the instructions of his constituency, so today a United States Senator may solemnly poll every second householder. But I am certain that Adams accounted it an important fact that when the town of Braintree instructed its representative, it did so by vote in open meeting, after the issues had been thoroughly hashed over. As for the modern politician's poll, the Senator himself frames the questions out of his own intimate knowledge of the problems and interests of his constituents; nor does he feel obliged to tell us what the results are, or how he will use them. But for those engaged in the direct sampling of opinions verbally expressed the assumptions of direct democracy provide a convenient rationale. When Dr. George Gallup lectured at Princeton in 1939 on "Public Opinion in a Democracy" he found representative processes inefficient because they failed to reveal the popular will with certainty. On the other hand, the pollster had demonstrated by his pre-election surveys that he could accurately measure public opinion, and could thus promptly give voice to the popular will. Aided by the opinion analyst at his elbow, the function of the statesman was simply that of discovering and implementing public opinion. It was apparent that the pollster had little patience with the problems which the theory of public opinion had posed for philosophers.

If the modern interest in public opinion is the direct outcome of the theory and practice of constituency representation, so is polling clearly in accord with the assumptions of direct democracy. But in political terms polling is also open to all of the criticisms to which the techniques of direct democracy were exposed, and I suspect, partly for this reason, that representative institutions will survive this as they did the earlier challenge.

PART  FIVE

A Region and a Tradition in Transition

THE SOUTH AND THE NEW FRONTIER

By RORERT S. CHAUVIN

Robert S. Chauvin is Professor of Geography at Stetson University. His major field of interest is historical Geography and Geopolitics. He is the co-author of GLOBAL GEOGRAPHY and OUTLINES OF WORLD ECONOMIC GEOGRAPHY.

"Had I two loaves of bread," said Mohammed, "I would sell one, and buy white hyacinths to feed my soul." This bit of oriental philosophy had a profound impact upon me when I was a boy growing up in northern New York state. It seemed to me then, that the gathering of hyacinths should be the main purpose of life, but in my life there appeared to be only weeds. There was poverty about, and in rural glacier-eroded New York state there seemed only stones to pick in summer and snow to shovel in winter. The future, viewed from the depths of the depression with eyes that had known little else, looked drab and unexciting. True, an occasional hyacinth did grace the landscape, but it appeared as something of an accident. The future seemed less than promising.

However, I knew, like every other young man in this environment knew, that there was indeed a land of the hyacinth—a land of mystery far away—the Southland, or Dixie. A land of the magnolia tree, with Negroes softly strumming banjos and singing at eventide —in harmony, of course—a never, never Beulah Land of milk and honey where stately mansions stood, graceful women danced in beautiful dresses, and young gentlemen pursued the fox and lived the genteel life. True, I had never known a Southerner, had never spoken to anyone who had even been within the southern region, but I was still acquainted with the traditions of this chivalrous, romantic, and genteel culture by way of the romantic novel. Why, oh why, had I been born among the weeds?

Time passed, the Second World War exploded, and because the Military specializes in transferring rookies to unfamiliar places, I was sent south. At last, Utopia! But my first observations of the southern region, confirmed by later experience, convinced me that all was not well in the land of the hyacinth, or, more appropriately, the magnolia. There were many weeds spread over the landscape, and some of these had roots reaching deep into the social soil; others had grown so high that they threatened to deface and even obliterate the landscape. Indeed, many visitors could see only weeds— segregation, poverty, conformity, corruption, fundamentalism. I learned, too, perhaps symbolically, that the hyacinth can be a scourge as it stops up rivers and streams, that beauty can sometimes beget evil.

But much time has elapsed since then. During this time the South has emerged as a new frontier. And just as the illusion of the hyacinth days faded into oblivion, the weed-filled landscape is also yielding to a better planned horticultural landscape. This new landscape is being carved out by the Southerner himself for the first time. He is taking his destiny into his own hands.

This then is the thesis I should like to explore in this essay; that the South is losing its stereotyped image, and its institutions and culture are merging into the mainstream of the American civilization of the 20th Century.

I

The single unifying geo-physical element of the region is the land—the soil, supplemented, to be sure, by a fairly uniform climate with sufficient rainfall and a long, warm, growing season. Although other physical elements— landforms, flora, minerals, water resources and fauna—vary greatly, the fact is that in resources the South is not a poor region. The cohesive force that unites these physical diversities and the people is the particular socio-cultural pattern which evolved in the region after the Civil War, along with the problems of soil exhaustion and, recently, the necessity for change. The experimental process by which other sections in the United States found their ecological status some years ago is being conducted here now, and the resulting transition has been rapid, especially since the Second World War.

This economic transition has taken advantage of science and research, a fact that has enabled the South to avoid the errors made by other regions in the United States as they passed through many stages of ecological succession. It is beginning to learn, too, something about the marshalling of its own abundant resources, the soils, the minerals, water power, flora, and, especially, its people. Thus, for the first time, there is evidence that the Southerner is beginning to adapt himself to his subtropical climate and soils and balance the uses of these with wise industrial development.

The changes occurring on the new Southern frontier may be

best understood when one surveys the recent trends in the two basic geographical elements of the region, the people and the land.

II

In 1960, the Southern region comprised about 25 percent of the nation's population, and throughout the twentieth century the population of the region has remained approximately at that percentage. There have been notable changes in the population patterns, however. One of the most striking of these is the exodus from the land and the accompanying rapid increase in urbanization. In 1950, 44.9 percent of the South was urban, but this percentage had risen to 55 by 1960, indicating that the rate of urban growth for the South exceeded that of any other region in the country. In addition, over 55 percent of the counties throughout Dixie lost population during the last decade, a rate well above the national average.

Another notable trend is the decreasing number of Negroes in the region. On the eve of the Civil War, 40 percent of the people in the Southern states were Negroes; in 1960 the percentage had dropped to about 20, and the trend has been one of continued steady decline. Migration of both whites and Negroes has always been a major factor in Southern population patterns. In fact, the region has long served the country as a reservoir of brains and brawn because the out-migration drained mature people from the area.

Hence, while the South boasts the largest number of young people within its population of any part of America, many of these persons do not remain into maturity. The new agricultural and industrial South should enable it to retain its citizens and allow them ample opportunity to make contributions to their emerging homeland.

Another feature of Southern population has been the large percentage of native born, indicating that few have migrated to this region. This, of course, exempts those retiring people coming to Florida for their "golden years."

The economic changes have brought a significant increase in the consumer purchasing power of most Southerners. The rise in income levels stems partly from the new industrial development, partly from the recent trends toward a diversified agriculture, but mainly from the better balancing of the two, which has greatly strengthened the general economy. Traditionally, the South catered to the production and exportation of a few staples, tobacco, rice, and especially cotton. It was necessary, therefore, to import into the

139

region commodities of industry and agriculture which the region did not furnish itself largely because of the devotion to the single cash crop—King Cotton. The resulting quasi-feudal economy was unbalanced and highly subject to the Achilles heel of all agrarian societies—fluctuating prices. Today these deficiencies are being eliminated. The South is still an exporter, but the export list consists of multiple products and many of these are consumed or used within the region.

As the general economy of the region has changed, so, too, have the work patterns. The number of workers engaged in agriculture has steadily declined— 32 percent in 1940, 21 percent in 1950, 18 percent in 1960—whereas the number engaged in industrial work has increased to 22 percent. Despite the increase in industrial workers, however, the South remains agrarian because the value of agricultural commodities continues to exceed that of industry.

The rapid development of manufacturing in the American South is based upon several types of enterprises. First, expansion has centered upon the traditional industries, textiles, naval stores, cotton-seed products, and tobacco. Secondly, such new and more sophisticated industries have become established as chemicals, synthetic rubber, refined petroleum products, electrical goods, metal goods, shipbuilding, electronic equipment and others. Thirdly, new by-product manufacturing, which is an old New England industrial characteristic, has been incorporated into the Southern industrial landscape. And lastly, defense industries supported by the Federal government have been established. Most manufactures of the South are termed "simple manufactures." That is, the manufactural process adds little value to the finished products. The list of newly established industries is long, but included among them are such diverse plants as the $600,000,000 H Bomb plant near Aiken, South Carolina, the Martin Company of Orlando, Florida, the General Electric branch in Daytona Beach, Florida, the General Motors and Ford automobile plants in Atlanta, Georgia, the Reynolds Aluminum Works in Baton Rouge, the Chemstrand Corporation Nylon Plant of Pensacola, Florida, and the huge Cape Kennedy complex in Florida.

The Gulf Coast has developed large chemical industries and the oil refineries long located there have been expanded. New iron and steel plants have been constructed during the last decade at Houston, Fort Worth, and Galveston, Texas. It is interesting to note that the well advertised and historically famous fall-zone along the Piedmont has received few of the new enterprises. Instead, the location of new industries tends to follow the ever-expanding urban centers where consumer purchasing power is creating demands within those city markets.

And, because the Southern region is large and encompasses many growing urban areas, the present industrial boom should continue throughout the forseeable future.

In 1955, John F. Kennedy, in an article for *Atlantic Monthly* observed that as early as 1951 the South was securing an average of one multi-million dollar factory each day. Since that time the factories have continued to come.

III

The potential of the New South as well as the misfortunes of the old can be easily envisioned by examining the land. The old, exhausted, depleted soil areas are being rejuvenated by such scientific farming techniques as diversified farming, crop rotation, contour plowing, and by introducing new grasses and cover crops which better fit the land and the climate. Commercial fertilizers are being used as never before. The Southern farmer is consuming presently about 53 percent of all the fertilizer in the nation.

Tenant farming, once a blight on the agricultural landscape, is disappearing rapidly. From a total of almost two million units in 1925, the number dropped to approximately 1.1 million in 1945, and has been reduced to 341,000 in 1960. And, significantly, as the number of farms decreased, there has been a trend toward larger farm units, thus insuring more efficient tilling and production.

The new trend toward diversification and improved practices in farming and husbandry has resulted in a remarkable rise in farm income. In 1940, farm income was $1,600,000,000. In 1960, it had reached an all-time peak of almost $6,000,000,000. Although some of this differential stems from rising prices during this 20-year period, most of the gain relates to the new transition. There has been a steady abandonment of the traditional crops, cotton and tobacco, and new interest has focused upon small grains, truck crops, ornamental plants, soybeans, hay and forage crops and peanuts. One of the most noteworthy trends of the new agrarian frontier is the expansion of the livestock industries. Twenty years ago few cattle grazed in Southern pastures. In fact, there were few pastures available in which they could forage. Today, the farmer has discovered the profit in raising beef cattle in an environment where general costs of production can be kept low. Horticulture, poultry farming, and the dairy industries are developing around the many mushrooming urban centers. Even so, however, these industries cannot parallel the urban rate of growth. Demand continues to outstrip the supply.

Tree farming has likewise become an industry of considerable import throughout the region. Over 50 percent of the South is forested; this growth represents approximately one-third of the nation's forests. At present, the South contributes well over half of the nation's timber, and, as the amount of timber decreases in other regions, the South, because of its silviculture program, will reap the benefits.

IV

The South, therefore, is not the number one economic problem of the United States any longer. An economic revolution is taking place and the Southerner himself is the prime mover. He is clearing the weeds from the fields and the newly planted crop is beginning to bloom.

But the revolution in aspects other than the economic is just beginning. When we examine the intellectual, political, and social portions of the frontier, we encounter the internal forces which retarded economic progress for so long. They are centered around the basic characteristics of the well-structured Southern society. I refer to those which I shall call the forces of conformity and fundamentalism. Their roots are deep and relate somewhat to the historical and institutional development of the region. But most of all, they have crystallized because all strata of society had two denominators which demanded their existence. One was the segregation of the Negro, and the other was the anti-Northern feeling. The poor white may have been as badly off economically and otherwise as his Negro neighbor over the hill, but he had one advantage. He was white, and because of this the restaurant served him and he could enter wherever he wished—privileges which set him conspicuously apart from the Negro. He had little else to bolster his self esteem, so of course he demanded that segregation remain. Other segments of the body "sociale" strove to maintain the status quo for equally timorous reasons. Many made the northern regions the "whipping boy" for all Southern ills.

The interesting and significant point here is that the new frontiersmen who are leading the revolt against conformity and fundamentalism are composed largely of internal forces rather than external ones, as was the case with the farmer. For example, the typical Southern state university was formerly a place where one could learn a trade, or acquire an education of sorts as long as he stayed within bounds and did not explore areas which were sacrosanct. Students might even use the college as a finishing school to learn the manners necessary for the making of ladies or gentlemen. But the academic community was safe. There were not many ideas running counter to the framework established and maintained firmly by the conformists and fundamentalists which were tolerated.

One has only to examine the record to find case after case illustrating how this worked. The numerous dismissals of professors and teachers for teaching evolution, or the many accused and fired as communists, can be well-documented. Perhaps the symbolic case concerns the dismissal of Homer Rainey as president of the University of Texas during the mid 1940's. The forces of conformity swept all before them. They had no hesitance in eliminating the dissenters either directly or through the legislatures they influenced.

But what is happening now? Since 1961 there have been cases involving academic freedom in the state university systems in almost every Southern state ranging from Texas to Virginia, and in practically every case the forces of pressure lost, partly because a new breed of scholar has arrived upon the academic scene. The new economic order is encouraging better endowed persons to enter and remain in teaching. As elsewhere, additional funds for the university systems are making these men restless for better libraries, more efficient equipment, and higher salaries. But most of all, they are now insisting upon their freedom to explore every area in their quest for truth.

Another important factor contributing to the failure of the forces of conformity and fundamentalism is public opinion. In our state of Florida when the Johns' Committee reported on the state of the University of South Florida, many Floridians rushed to the defense of the college and forced the committee to retreat after many of its investigatory functions and rights had been curtailed. The fact that so many cases have arisen is evidence enough that revolt is being generated within the hallowed halls. And further, this revolt is often led by Southerners, some of whom have labored for years in the classrooms and laboratories. It has been something of a shock to the forces of conformity to find some men who were once lambs suddenly become lions.

Because the Southern state university has suffered historically from a lack of challenge, I suppose one could say with some degree of truth that the entrance of James Meredith into the University of Mississippi served more than the cause of integration. He presented a challenge to an academic community that had long needed one. His entrance and its consequences required the entire academic community to become involved in a situation together that called for considerable thinking, soul searching, and decision making. The University of Mississippi will always be a better institution because of this crisis.

As part of this new intellectual frontier the old fear of science with its accompanying implications is passing away. I doubt if there are many accredited colleges and universities within the region today which do not teach evolution and read Darwin, although the word evolution may be well camouflaged or seldom used.

A short time ago I had an interesting but almost incredible conversation with a genuine conformist, an old man who is incidentally a prominent citizen of our state. It began when he noticed a copy of Darwin's *Descent and Origin* on my desk.

"I suppose you've read that," he observed. I confessed that I had.

"What did you think of it?" he asked. I successfully evaded the question and an inevitable argument by saying that the book had had a profound impact upon social philosophy and scientific investigation.

"Well, I don't put much stock in it," he replied. "If evolution is a fact why aren't rabbits or monkeys changing into men now? And why aren't we changing into other colors besides black and white?"

From this illogical statement one can see easily the incomprehensibility of the subject at this level. But two years ago when a religious group attempted to hold meetings for the purpose of withdrawing children from the Dade County schools because evolution was being taught, people were amused and very few attended the meetings. The project died for lack of interest. So perhaps there is some vestige of hope.

Everyday living in a scientific age and the application of scientific methods to earn his daily bread has done much to further the acceptance of science by the individual. And, of course, the university revolt that has demanded the right to conduct research freely has done much to further the cause.

The media of communication, especially television, has brought the rapidly exploding world of scientific phenomena closer to all. It is difficult to reject what one sees. Also, the Southerner has always been passionately nationalistic as well as provincial, and science is the new weapon with which America can defeat all enemies. So it must be good, indeed it must be sacred. And, don't you know, we must beat the Russians to the moon, develop better and more efficient means of destruction. So, says the conformist, we must accept science and steep the next generation in it, whatever it costs—whatever the consequences.

The same changes are being experienced in the area of the Arts. A region almost devoid of aesthetics since the Civil War, the South is now becoming art conscious. Today art galleries are springing up, symphony orchestras are being sponsored in most of the larger cities, and books are being written and read as never before. A frontier fosters the growth of writers, and significant among those on the Southern scene are the increasing numbers of Negro writers. They have written largely out of their regional experience of bitterness and protest, but recently there have been signs of a shift away from this and toward more of an involvement in American life. Negro writings are very much in demand now; the publishing business is said to be in a "Negro phase" much as it was in a "gray flannel phase" a few years ago.

In political thought, trends indicate that the new frontier may differ radically from the old. Because of the new economic trends, the developing intellectual revolution, and the recent action of the United States Supreme Court, a new development is about to take place which will chart the future political course of the Southern region. I refer to the apportionment of the State Legislatures. With apportionment the old agrarian control probably disappears, and a new group, the urban proletariat and the city dweller, assumes authority. Urban forces have traditionally tended to be less conservative than rural ones in the South, though there are notable exceptions. Birmingham stands out as one, especially when compared with progressive Atlanta. The old stump speaker and others rallying the forces of fundamentalism and conformity by rattling the swords of segregation may begin to find their weapons tarnished.

The trend away from rural authority is already discernible in some areas of the South, and perhaps by the next decade urban influence will be well established. The former gubernatorial candidate who compaigned recently with the following line will probably disappear. This man said, "All Negroes who crusade for change and those whites who support them are Communists or parts of a Communist plot to wreck our way of life."

So the Claghorns will probably drift gradually from the offices at the state and national levels, but I suspect there will be a few always representing some poverty pockets—the poverty not necessarily stemming from economic deprivation. On the local level, they will be with us for a long time to come, despite the newly rising urban authority. They will probably continue to preach local rights, little suspecting that the rights they purport to uphold are meagre indeed, and often such that one thanks God that there is a Federal government and a Federal court system which gives a citizen recourse against the local interpretation of what they are. When local rights are spoken of, what is usually meant is the right of the forces of conformity and reaction to demand that everyone within the community follow the old set of attitudes and conform to them. By Federal interference is really meant the breaking of the pattern by external forces. The implication here is that all rights and privileges stem from the local authority, and that the Federal Government is a lion to be greatly feared—a supposition that does not always bear up well under scrutiny. Local rights and its big brother States' Rights, really deal little with constitutional factors, but are devices to maintain the status quo and to wall the Yankee and integrationist out, because somehow the Federal Government is equated with Yankees and integrationists. This attitude of suspicion is especially applied to the United States Supreme Court.

One reason for the lagging development of labor unions in the South is that they are mentally associated with Northern activities. The organizer is usually from the North and when he enters a Southern community to organize workers he is regarded with considerable suspicion and resistance. The unions are related, also, to Northern values, many of which run counter to those of the Southern conformist.

The Federal Government has, however, made its encroachment into the life of the Southerner somewhat more bearable by the outlay of gigantic expenditures for the construction of roads, hospitals, schools, and installations of various other kinds—national defense or industrial in character. Even the most ardent States' Righter must realize that as part of the new frontier, the Federal Goverment will play a larger role than ever in its relations with him, and no state can secede financially from the Federal structure.

As part of the new South then, there will be recognition that the United States Federal Government is here to stay, is solvent when the state may not be, and that really the theory of State's rights, interposition, and the like, are of little consequence. In fact, as time passes these issues will bring fewer and fewer votes.

On the political frontier the two party system will probably develop. If, as David Potter suggests, one of the weaknesses of the Southern political tradition has been caused by the lack of a two-party system, we can expect this weakness to be strengthened. The caliber of the candidates for office will probably improve and in so doing push the remaining Claghorns out of public office.

Historically, the South has served as a great laboratory for teaching the biology of disease. But the diseases once rampant— hookworm, yellow fever, malaria—have been controlled. Higher living standards will enable the Southerner to spend more money on preventive medicine and to enjoy a healthier and longer life.

But if the South has contributed greatly to the biology of disease, so has it also served as a laboratory for the study of diet. A former gubernatorial candidate once entertained prospective voters by saying, "If one of them high collared fly weight dudes of the East had sense enough to set down to a big dish of turnip greens, Poke 'sallet' and hog jowl he might sweat off enough of that talcum powder to look like a man." Though few people today would champion such fare, the fact remains that a large segment of the population still suffers from malnutrition. A diet of pork, corn bread, and cane syrup or molasses, is still the fare of many, not always because more healthful food is not available, but some times because the people eat what their parents did and what they have learned to like. Because their health is poor, and their energy low, they are in effect slowly starving to death from lack of protein and other nutritious foods. Often the problem is augmented by the drinking of hard liquor. The problem, then, is to an extent one of educating the people to being more diet and health conscious, a project that is already underway in the classrooms and school lunchrooms as well as the country level. Fewer and fewer people would appreciate or even understand the candidate's remark about poke "sallet." The traditional Southern dish of hog jowl and poke salad will soon pass the way of the Model T Ford and New England bundling customs, except perhaps as a tourist dish.

Another problem which the New South must face concerns the use of leisure time. As technology advances, more and more time is released to the individual. On the farm, in the factory, in the home, machinery is cutting down on the human work force required. Particularly in the textile industry, where much cheap labor has been employed both in the factories and in the fields, the machines are moving in. And the people thrown out of work are usually those that are least equipped to make adjustments. The New South will not spurn the Federal Government's efforts to rehabilitate these citizens as part of its anti-poverty drive. Indeed, it will welcome them and any other programs that will save her human resources.

What can we say about the cult of womanhood that crystallized throughout the South? The woman was the very symbol of conformity in a sense, standing serenely on a pedestal. It has been suggested that the Southern male put her there, using the protection of her purity as a rationale for his stand on segregation. His guilt feelings on that issue might be relieved considerably if they could be related to the protection of his women's virtue. Although women accepted the prestige and leisure this role cast upon them, there is evidence that the limitations sometimes chafed. There were some rebels, but the cult persisted until the Second World War when women donned overalls to work in the war plants or uniforms to serve in the military forces. Her aura dissipated, and she was now ready to take her place in the man's world. Although she still has a long way to go in securing equal salaries and opportunities, she has gone far toward that goal in two decades. The fact that Margaret Chase Smith is running for president is significant not only for Southern women, but for all women.

I do not mean to imply that all women in every area of the South were part of this system of chivalry. Many on small farms and in the backwoods toiled hard and long both inside and out, with little or no recognition or appreciation. The new frontier will bring a better deal for them and perhaps enable them to enjoy some of the leisure of which their sisters had too much.

V

The effects of a region in transition have implications for the churches, too. The two major churches of the South, the Baptist and the Methodist, are beginning to experience change. At one time in Southern history, I imagine, it was difficult to distinguish between them. To be sure, there were theological differences such as methods of baptism and others, but services and doctrines were generally similar. As George Harmon suggests in "Harper's" a Baptist could feel at home in a Methodist church and vice versa. Apparently little effort was made to convert Baptists to the Methodist Church, and despite the evangelism of the Baptist movement, Methodists were regarded as Christian brothers and sisters. Both churches, as Harmon observes, were concerned about the doctrines of Catholics and Jews, and both dispatched missionaries to far away places to convert the heathen. But the point is that if a Baptist boy married a Methodist girl no great excitement was generated. Ministers often exchanged pulpits.

Today, however, the Methodist Church of the South has changed radically. More and more emphasis is being placed upon social change and attention is being focused upon social questions of the new frontier. In a sense this should not be surprising because the church itself was a product of social change. The social gospel has always been an integral part of its nature. Another reason, states Harmon, centers around the centralized form of its government. It is a single federated church, and because the northern and southern branches merged in 1939, it has had 25 years of experience as a national church to think nationally about America's social and economic problems.

It is not surprising, therefore, to find Methodists encouraging teenagers to discuss proper sex behavior or problems concerning alcohol in a church where such talk was once taboo. Nor is one amazed to read about the church's interest and leadership in such modernistic problems as foreign relations, segregation, unionism, and world peace. The recent trend in Methodism in the South has also been toward a large church. It is felt that a church program can meet the needs of all its members only if it can provide a multi-purpose program.

The Baptist church, on the other hand, has tended to be less responsive to changing conditions in the South. The primary reason for this appears to lie in the Evangelical nature of the church. The Baptist Church has tended to remain regional in character because it is decentralized in organization. Each church is an independent unit. The Southern Baptist Convention is but a confederation of totally independent churches. The Baptist cherishes this type of organization because he feels it is compatible with his heritage of freedom and democracy. And, because evangelism is crucial to his belief, he prefers the small congregation. Indeed, many Baptists feel no church should exceed 500-600 members. Instead, new churches or missions should be established constantly from the larger congregations.

But despite these factors there are signs of transition among the Baptist groups, too. Recently, throughout the South there has been a trend toward the construction of larger, grander Baptist churches to correspond with the improving financial status of the members. The clergy is becoming better educated and perhaps more sophisticated and less fundamental. One must not forget, either, that during the past three years, like the state universities, the seminaries have heard some dissenting voices. Dissenting professors in the theological schools, although accomplishing little now, must eventually lead to a reevaluation of church doctrine, organization, and theology. It is a fact that the seeds of change are growing in the Baptist soil also.

VI

The American South has had a history colored by strife and valor. What is happening today throughout the region could never have come about except for the unique history that has gone before. The Golden Age of the South lies yet ahead. New hyacinths and magnolias are sprouting in the ready soil. However, before this age can arrive, the horticulturist must turn his energies toward plucking from the garden the rankest and bitterest weed of all— segregation. If he accomplishes this, as he must, the new Southern frontier, unlike most frontiers that have often trammeled democratic rights, will become a laboratory where regional change occurs through the operation of Democratic processes.

The American people may be on the threshold of a new frontier. If so, the Southern region can find itself in a unique position of leadership and could chart the course for the future of the entire American nation. The opportunity is there; only inertia can block the way.

THE ROMANTIC HERITAGE AND
AMERICAN CHARACTER

By John A. Hague

John A. Hague is a graduate of the American Studies program at Yale University. He is Professor of the Charles E. Merrill Program of American Studies at Stetson University in DeLand, Florida. His articles have been concerned with recent intellectual history and studies of American character. He is currently working on a biography of the late Charles Nagel.

In 1858 Oliver Wendell Holmes celebrated Puritanism's demise by describing the collapse of the deacon's wonderful shay. One hundred years later American writers, responding to the tensions of the cold war and the machine age, were noting the collapse of romantic attitudes and ideals which had held sway in the nineteenth century. Arthur Winner, the protagonist in a novel by James Gould Cozzens, discovered that his legal ethics and personal values could not easily mesh. By contrast, his father had never known such a conflict. Seemingly Americans were experiencing a loss of innocence. The collapse of romantic idealism appeared real and complete.

We now know that Puritanism did not die in 1858. It had stepped out for a change of clothes, but it was by no means stripped of its influence. Indeed twentieth century scholars have rediscovered both its influence and its value. In the nineteen forties, for example, Ralph Barton Perry wrote a large opus which proclaimed the impact of Puritanism and democracy on American life. Perry astutely noted the ways in which these traditions reinforced each other as well as the ways in which they clashed. He pointed out that America's debt to both traditions was large.

Similarly, one wonders if romanticism is really dead. Certainly some of the values and attitudes which it fostered are in jeopardy, but evidence of its influence can be found almost everywhere in American culture today. It is my purpose in this paper to define the nature and impact of romanticism on American character. Such an analysis will, I believe, provide some insights about the serviceability of the romantic heritage in the twentieth century. Specifically, it may indicate the general direction the romantic American's education ought to take.

I

In the nineteenth century a romantic tradition found fertile soil on a developing continent and succeeded in modifying the legacy of the preceding centuries. In order to understand American romanticism let us examine briefly two movements which did much to define its tone. Frontier evangelism, on the one hand, and transcendentalism, on the other, furnished the context out of which lasting romantic influences sprang. The evangelical religion of the frontier was a response to the insecurities and loneliness of the frontiersman's life. The evangelist preached a gospel of love, redemption and salvation. He called upon sinners to forsake their evil ways, to wash in the blood of the lamb and become "as white as snow." The impact of the resulting conversion experience transfigured the frontiersman's life. Beholding a vision of a future life in a golden city, he went back to his farm to live courageously "at" his future rather than "in" the present. His life, regardless of the physical circumstances which surrounded it, had acquired a new significance and a heroic dimension.

The transcendentalists were also intent on tapping the spiritual resources of the human condition. They too had conversion experiences, although they were less likely to refer to a single and total transformation than were the pioneering farmers. Nevertheless, they found within themselves, in those moments when they touched the oversoul, a sense of wholeness and strength which filled the present with a spark of eternity. Such experiences persuaded the transcendentalists that greatness was a state of being and that life was a journey in which the traveler constantly searched for the heroic virtues. Although the heroic virtues arose from the spiritual self-reliance of the individual, most transcendentalists expected men to translate these virtues into lives of useful service. Emerson could not completely conceal a tinge of exasperation when he thought of Thoreau captaining a huckleberry party.

A number of conditions aided and abetted the growth of a romantic outlook. Men were conquering a continent—in an unbelievably short span of time. In the process they had to be self-reliant and daring. Secondly, America was engaged, in the words of Walt Rostow, in its drive to maturity. Americans were applying a growing technology to all sectors of the economy, and many witnessed in their own lifetime the full impact of the industrial revolution. Third, it was a century of mass migration to the new world. Nearly sixty million Europeans left Europe in the nineteenth century, and approximately thirty-six million settled in the United States. The image of the melting pot is not altogether accurate, but we can recognize that the availability of sizeable rewards created a pressure on the immigrant to strive for success that was virtually irresistible. Many people argued that it was the influx of new blood that gave America her strength and vitality.

II

David Riesman has noted many of these factors in describing the "inner directed" American. The inner directed style of conformity was presumably in its heyday during the late nineteenth and early twentieth centuries. Riesman cited the fact that the inner directed individual was success oriented and therefore work oriented. Since his work had to do with problems related to industrialization or the agricultural conquest of the continent, the inner directed man typically found himself engaged in hard physical labor. He took vacations in order to work more effectively, and he strove to achieve an ever higher status in the community. His source of strength came from the values which the community instilled and subsequently rewarded.

Riesman's concepts of tradition, inner and other directed modes separated work from play, adults from children, and social classes from each other in a clear cut fashion. As a result the inner directed society had a sense of direction and purpose which reflected the clearly defined class lines and values it contained. Riesman argued further that the images of power coincided pretty closely with the actualities of power in the nineteenth century.

Riesman's concepts of tradition, inner and other directed modes of conformity are models, just as the second law of thermodynamics is a model. The real question which we must ask about his models is how useful are they? Do they help us understand more clearly and precisely the reasons for the responses which we have made and are making? In this instance does the concept of inner direction provide a useful key to understanding the behavior of the "romantic" American of the late nineteenth century?

Its usefulness is decidedly limited. Carl Degler has already observed that a good deal of evidence points to the conclusion that Americans have always been other directed.[1] In addition, I

---

[1] Carl N. Degler, "The Sociologist as Historian: Riesman's, *The Lonely Crowd*" *American Quarterly* (Winter, 1963) Vol. XV, Number 4. pp. 483-497.

believe that other factors explain more carefully and fully the behavioral responses which Riesman has noted. Many of Riesman's insights are remarkably fruitful, but the model itself is a trifle suspect.

Before I examine the "other" factors I think it is well to point out that Riesman's models were designed primarily to explain middle and uppermiddle class behavior. With this I have no quarrel. A great many observers have insisted that America has consistently demonstrated a fondness for middle class values, and Americans themselves have been quick to apply the label to their own position in society.

The fact remains, however, that the nineteenth century middle class was a much smaller group, both absolutely and relatively, than its twentieth century counterpart. As a result, when we talk about the inner directed middle classes of a previous generation we are talking about a fairly restricted group that defined its status in rather explicit terms. Success meant a house in the right neighborhood, the requisite number of servants, the right kind of household furnishings, and membership in the respectable community organizations and churches. Under these circumstances one can readily appreciate what Carl Becker meant when he said, shortly after the turn of the century, that American individualism was marked by achievement rather than eccentricity, by conformity rather than revolt.[2]

When Riesman began to examine twentieth century American society he discovered that individuals were often directed with reference to the groups in which they were participating. Thus the bohemians of Greenwich Village, far from being highly individualistic, were other directed with reference to each other. In other words, these individuals discovered a group whose approval they needed and coveted. The evidence seems to indicate a similar state of affairs with reference to the inner directed middle classes of the earlier period. When Sinclair Lewis created George Babbitt in 1920, he portrayed a middle class businessman who finally admitted to himself that he simply could not subsist without the approval of his peers. One can argue, of course, that Babbitt symbolizes neatly the emergent other directed character structure, but his upbringing and community ties suggest strongly a middle class, inner directed value profile.

One factor which explains a good deal about the responses of nineteenth century Americans, as well as twentieth century Ameri-

[2]Carl L. Becker, "Kansas," reprinted in *Everyman His Own Historian* (New York: F. S. Crofts & Co., 1905) p. 9.

cans, is their constant struggle to be upwardly mobile. To be mobile in a production oriented society one must work long and hard at the process. For Americans just entering the ranks of the middle classes leisure was almost non-existent. It is not hard to separate work and leisure when leisure is such a rare commodity to begin with. Some confined leisure to Saturday afternoons, and others, living in more isolated areas, combined leisure and religion once a year in a week long revival.

In 1900 a majority of Americans still lived in rural areas or in small towns and villages. Frederick Lewis Allen has pointed out that middle class Americans, prior to the first world war, did remarkably little traveling.[3] When one combines these facts with the observation that middle class status was a minority status, one gains additional insight into the homogeneous character of this group. Parents separated the adult world from the child world because they felt confident about their ability to retain control of the socialization process in which their children were participating. A child who could handle father's inquiry about where he'd been by saying "Out," and then dispose of "What did you do?" by replying "Nothing," was part of a social structure father knew and understood.

Perhaps this gets to the heart of the matter. Cora DuBois argues that four value premises underlie American middle class behavior. In brief, "(1) the universe is mechanistically conceived, (2) man is its master, (3) men are equal, and (4) men are perfectible."[4] One does not need to idealize the circumstances under which the middle classes toiled. Their lives had a grubby side and a dull side, and they longed unmistakably for a better day. But they believed that life, in the general sense, was manageable; that those who understood what they wanted and made proper use of their talent would secure their just deserts. In short a manageable world was one in which men were capable of creating and maintaining the conditions under which people got what they deserved.

As a result of this attitude, the middle class American maintained a strong personal orientation in most of his value judgments. Christopher Newman, the protagonist of Henry James' novel, *The American,* made a determined effort to get the aristocratic Bellegardes to disregard tradition and to evaluate his suit for their daughter on its own merits. Huck Finn made his decision to go

---

[3]Frederick Lewis Allen, *The Big Change* (New York: Harper & Brothers, 1952) pp. 7-8.

[4]Cora DuBois, "The Dominant Profile of American Culture," *American Anthropologist,* Vol. 57, Number 6, Part 1, (December, 1955) p. 1233.

to Hell on the basis of his personal loyalty to Jim. And few nine-teenth century Americans would have understood the novel that Melville completed at the century's close. In *Billy Budd* Melville produced a "romantic-tragic" book which juxtaposed the sympa-thetic individualism of the romanticist with the detached imperson-alism of the tragedian. Appropriately the book was not published until 1924.

It is perfectly true that many American businessmen were be-ginning to think in corporate terms. Rockefeller's willingness to sacrifice individual buds for the sake of the larger, more perfect bloom is a case in point. By and large, however, the personal orien-tation prevailed. Despite all of the differences which separated the New Nationalism of Theodore Roosevelt and the New Freedom of Woodrow Wilson, both men took strong personal views of the economy. Wilson wanted to make it possible for individuals to com-pete with corporations, and Roosevelt wanted to hold corporations accountable to a personal ethic. The speeches of both were redolent with phrases which reflected a personalized ethic.

In 1912 the good ship *Titanic* left England on its maiden voy-age to the United States. The ship was unsinkable. Thus it symbo-lized man's ultimate triumph over nature. Walter Lord has given us a dramatic account of the ship's last hours in the icebound North Atlantic. What is of significance for our purposes is the fact that the tragedy was made possible and then compounded because no one acted on the assumption that the ship could sink. The crew of a nearby vessel, seeing the distress flares of the *Titanic,* assumed that the passengers of the stricken vessel were having a celebration, be-cause the *Titanic* could not be in trouble. Such an assumption was logical if one believed that he lived in a knowable and manageable world. Proceeding on such an assumption one expected nature to be harnessed. One expected the growth of knowledge to reduce the hazards of daily life and to make more certain the achievement of the good society. We recognize today that Karl Marx was one of the great optimists about human nature in the nineteenth century. But he was not alone. Emerson, Thoreau, Henry George, and many others had their own concept of the withering away of the state, and their hopes for a brave new world ran high.

Perhaps enough has been said to provide a significant summary of the late nineteenth century middle class American and his atti-tudes. He strove for upward mobility and his life was work-oriented. Because of the context in which he lived and worked, he separated adult activities from child activities and also work from leisure. His individualism was an individualism of conformity rather than one of eccentricity. His value orientation was personal rather than corporate, provincial rather than cosmopolitan; and the symbols which denoted success seemed clearly defined. Living in a manageable world, he was prepared to make an heroic effort to achieve his goals. His goals, of course, were for the most part those which society wanted him to want. His response to success or failure, joy or sorrow, happiness or despair was highly personal, and his behavior reflected warmth and compassion or coldness and indifference, depending on the individual circumstances which prevailed.

Since the world was supposed to be knowable and manageable, the American labeled the forces and events which threatened to disrupt his world as immoral. He regarded the outbreak of war in Europe in 1914 with disbelief and horror, and described it in terms of barbarism and backsliding. Even those Americans, like James and Dewey, who rebelled against the absolutes with which conservatives sought to defend the status quo, insisted upon man's ability to control his fate.

As a result, the American moralized and romanticized his choices. By these terms I mean first, that he tended to decide matters on a black and white basis, and, second, that he did not examine critically the probable consequences of his choices. From this conclusion I draw two inferences. First, the American, as of 1914, had little reason or wish to criticize the direction in which he believed his society was going. Second, he was in no sense introspective about his convictions or his role in society. If these inferences are accepted, the likelihood that his individualism was one of conformity is accentuated.

Such a complex of attitudes and values made the American inventive, shrewd, and practical on a short run basis, and helpless, naive, and unrealistic on a long range basis. I am contending that it was not simply the frontier that made the American inventive, shrewd, and practical. These traits resulted from the American's preoccupation with short range and manageable problems. Henry Ford's biography provides a case in point. Few industrialists have been more ingenious than he. Yet, the very qualities which brought him such magnificent success almost brought about the destruction of the company he founded. His failure to assess the developing trends within American industry made the formulas by which he built up the Ford Motor Company a millstone for his executives. Thus the American's shortsightedness has frequently petrified his inventiveness and practicality. As far back as 1830 de Tocqueville was noting the tendency of Americans to generalize readily on the basis of quick success and limited experience.

What are the principal changes which the twentieth century has brought about? First, it has seemingly crowned American efforts with very great success. At least in a material sense Americans have been able to achieve many of the things which nineteenth century orators held out as the symbols of the good life. In a remarkably short period of time Americans have transformed their living conditions, their life expectancy, and their position as a world power. Second, the ranks of the middle class have been greatly enlarged. No longer is the middle class a minority group which can easily secure hired help. Third, Americans have become far more mobile, both physically and socially, than ever before. Only five per cent of the American people occupied the same dwelling in 1960 that they inhabited in 1940. The average real income of the bottom four-fifths of American families doubled between 1940 and 1960. Fourth, the stream of immigrants has dried up to a mere trickle. As one might expect, the problems of the American city and the American school have accordingly changed. Fifth, the public school, particularly the public high school, has come of age as an institution. It now serves a greater percentage of the population, and finds itself subject to a wider variety of demands and standards. Sixth, the twentieth century is in the process of becoming an age of automation and cybernation. In consequence the traditional institutions of work and property no longer fulfill their historic roles. The evidence clearly seems to support the conclusion that an increasing number of people will have to define their work along radically different lines. It also suggests that the possession of property no longer supplies an individual with a meaningful stake in society. Rather it is the possession of an education which furnishes the individual that stake. Seventh, the twentieth century has witnessed the development of bureaucracy and the centralization of power. Put another way this is an era which has attained elements of a corporate society. Eighth, the mass media of communication have tied the American people together in a way that was never before possible. In an age which has made a wide variety of goods and services available to the American people, their instruments of communication have, paradoxically, tightened the bonds of conformity. Similarly, in an age which has produced more and better education for increasing numbers of people, the media, by virtue of the huckster's persistent effort to reach the lowest common denominator, have forced an almost continual oversimplification of ideas and issues. Ninth, the physical frontiers of American society have closed, as Frederick Jackson Turner said they would. While few would question that significant opportunities remain, many would assert that they are sometimes hard to find. Others insist that the growth rate of a mature society must slow down, and that Americans ought to adjust to the fact. David Potter, for example, has suggested that modern society does not need so many highly mobile individuals, and that it may be possible to strike a different balance between the demands of mobility and those of status.[5] Tenth, for many Americans the twentieth century has brought fragmentation and alienation. Finally, the twentieth century has become an era in which war has become total and in a sense permanent. Walter Lippmann has pointed out that modern man has learned that war is not rational and that he cannot make peace. Thus he must learn to live with frustration.

IV

Before appraising the impact of these developments on the romantic tradition, I want to say a word about intellectual developments which have shaped the twentieth century mind all over the Western world. Intellectually the twentieth century citizen is the heir of Darwin, Freud, and Einstein. There are many, many consequences of these three revolutions of which we are still only vaguely aware, but it seems clear that they have extended our intellectual horizons, and that they have complicated forever the forces we must understand in order to discipline our lives intelligently. We cannot help being aware of the fact that we live in a particular culture, operate on fallible assumptions, and act with limited vision. The knower knows that he cannot dissociate what he knows from the concepts he used to discover the knowledge, and that the concepts were in turn shaped by a culture which he inherited. Rheinhold Neibuhr suggests an awareness of such facts when he argues that it is man's nature to seek an ultimate meaning and his fate to see every meaning which he achieves threatened.[6] Under such circumstances man is enjoined to accept his relativity which is to say his finiteness and his mortality.

The list of changes cited above is not intended to be exhaustive. It may, however, give us a basis upon which to make a comparison between the late nineteenth century middle class American and his mid-twentieth century counterpart. Many twentieth century Amer-

[5]David M. Potter, *People of Plenty* (Chicago: University of Chicago Press, 1954), p. 109.

[6]William Hordern, *A Layman's Guide to Protestant Theology* (New York: The Macmillan Company, 1955), p. 152.

icans are probably less work-oriented than their predecessors. They are apparently just as bound by conformity, although they travel more, read more, and have a wider range of choice when it comes to purchasing goods and services. The choice is wider both because of what is being produced and because of what people have to spend. Simultaneously the middle classes have become greatly enlarged. In the process the symbols which denote success have lost their clarity, and individuals have begun to work harder at the business of securing acceptance of the credentials they have already earned. DeTocqueville warned that in a democratic society the bonds of affection would be extended but relaxed. The twentieth century American has witnessed the extension of said bonds, and he has also seen them become increasingly superficial. The existential search for identity has become more difficult, and so the American has frequently sought identity through a conformity marked by its totality and its compulsiveness.

David Riesman has correctly pointed out that the totality of the conformity has made it difficult for the individual to separate his work and leisure, and it has also made it difficult for him to find constructive channels of escape. In Riesman's terminology it is difficult for the other-directed citizen to turn off his radar set.

The roots of alienation in the modern world spread out over a wide territory. I believe that one important sector into which the roots reach is the romantic traditon itself. The romantic's search for truth and meaning frequently led him to rebel against form and tradition. His quest also caused him to turn in upon himself and to begin an existential journey in pursuit of an inner and spiritual truth. In the nineteenth century romantics like Emerson and Thoreau were supported by a community with which they had personal ties. Later on a writer like Mark Twain discovered that the supporting community was disappearing and that he was left more and more to depend solely upon his own endeavors. As the support of the community faded, the burden of the existential journey grew increasingly heavy. In the twentieth century the romantic found little support in form, tradition, or community, and his rebellion often took on a pathetic or ridiculous character.

I would hazard a guess that the value orientation of the twentieth century American remains personal, although, as the preceding analysis suggests, he finds himself subject to a great many corporate structures and pressures. There is an interesting contrast between the personally oriented statements of most college and university catalogues and the impersonal operation of their bureaucracies. The American's value orientation has, however, shed a good deal of its provinciality, and has undoubtedly become somewhat more tolerant of other points of view.

The American's world is both manageable and unmanageable. It is manageable in the sense that he achieves on a day by day basis many of the immediate objectives which he pursues. His life span is increasing, and he secures transportation, education, and recreation for himself and the members of his household. Yet he is not immune to accidents; he is not impervious to boredom, and he is most decidedly not immune to the big bomb. He is not at all sure that he can translate his more or less sucessful management of daily life into successful management of the world scene. Furthermore, he finds that few choices are clear cut. He has to live with ambiguity and frustration. He is a man with a headache that won't go away.

Caught in such a predicament, some Americans have begun to wonder if they have been pursuing the right goals. The circumstances which have surrounded them with indecision and boredom have forced them to become introspective—to undertake the existential journey. Others rebel and follow prophets like Barry Goldwater and Norman Vincent Peale who assure them that life is not complicated, and that the goals are clear after all. Such men evoke an image of an earlier, simpler America, and exert an emotional appeal based on a romantic dream world which they themselves inhabit.

That we have been a goal seeking people is clear. Whether the goals themselves remain clear is another question. The search for goals, or purpose, or identity betrays a basic anxiety on the part of the American people. We have reached so many of the goals we have pursued that we are a little puzzled about where we should go next. After World War II Americans confronted a crisis in Europe and in the developing nations. We responded quickly, and the period which gave birth to the Marshall Plan, the North Atlantic Alliance, and the Point Four Program will surely rank as one of the most creative in the history of our foreign affairs. Since that time, however, our policies appear to have grown more rigid, and we have displayed increasing uncertainty in our efforts to cope with conditions around the globe. When the Russians lanuched the first Sputnik Americans began an all-out effort to match the Russian space age scientific achievements. In summer of 1964 this effort appears to have been remarkably successful, and simultaneously we seem to be somewhat at a loss in planning our next moves. Walt Rostow has already noted that Americans may be becoming somewhat bored with the miracle of high mass consumption. His observation simply underscores the fact that people who build their lives on the attainment of finite goals are likely to have a sense of emptiness when they reach their objective. How many novelists never overcame a first success? What would have happened to William Faulkner if Yoknapatawpha County had integrated in 1938, or in 1929? Like the bear that went over the mountain we now know that there is not a garden of Eden on the other side. There is just another mountain. Moreover, the mountains are getting harder to climb.

V

Can the romantic heritage serve us in some fashion in such a time? Serve us it must, since it is part of our very beings. But it must adapt to the changed context of the twentieth century. I believe that three major adaptions are required. First romanticism must be disciplined by a sense of tragedy. There is a meaningful link between nineteenth century romanticism and twentieth century existentialism, and, on the surface at least, there is no incompatibility between romanticism and tragedy.

Lincoln managed the combination in the nineenth century. Scott Buchanan, in a discussion published by The Center for the Study of Democratic Institutions, argues that "power politics is tragic in its life course."[7] The beginning of political wisdom, he continues, lies in an understanding of Oedipus Rex. The highpoint of the play comes when Oedipus discovers that he himself is the criminal for whom he has been searching. "Everything he had done had a double meaning which now began to be disclosed. And finally the tragic fact came out that he was the criminal. He thereupon destroyed his sight and said, 'I see.' "[8] The world, concludes Buchanan, needs the wisdom of Oedipus.

> If you don't know that there is going to be a calamity, you are a silly, pathetic person. If you do know there is going to be a calamity and you just accept it, you are silly again. The only way to make it mean something is to be heroic about it. But the heroism is not the heroism of the Nazis—what they called realistic heroism, where you act heroic as a big gesture. You don't do that; you just discover things, and it makes life noble and grand while it is happening.[9]

Buchanan is asserting that the heroic vision can be combined with the tragic vision.

---

[7]Center For the Study of Democratic Institutions, "Tragedy and the New Politics" (Santa Barbara, The Fund For the Republic, 1960), p. 21.

[8]*Ibid.,* p. 21.

[9]*Ibid.,* p. 22.

George Santayana said much the same thing in his only novel, *The Last Puritan.* Oliver Alden finally comes to recognize that his friends will never thank or repay him for the gifts he bestows. Neither will he forsake his duty, even when it requires that he lay down his life. The romantic tragedean understands and accepts the necessity of commitment to imperfect causes. He recognizes the necessity of striving for perfection at the same time that he accepts the fact that he cannot reach it. He knows, but is never complacent about, the fact that men do not always get what they deserve. He has something of the quality which Christopher Newman, in James' *The American,* shows when he refuses to exact an "eye for an eye" from the Bellegardes. He has something of the quality which George Webber displays in *You Can't Go Home Again* when he refuses to accept the notion that something or even anything is impossible. Yet he knows that only a little *is* possible.

The second adaptation involves the capacity to appraise realistically the world in which man lives. The American must examine critically the events and movements which surround him, and he must acquire as much and as precise information as he can about social structures and the way people interact with them.

The third adaptation involves the perspective of the romantic. He must acquire a sense of history which he has rarely had. For he must learn to set the short view against the long view, and he cannot do this until he comes to terms with his own past. Jack Burden, in *All the King's Men,* finally accepts the burden of his past because he discovers that one cannot hope for the future until he accepts the past. In short one must both understand and *accept* the past in order to assess what is possible in the present and in the future.

The romantic who attempts these adaptations will discover that he needs self-discipline and self-knowledge. He will need to measure carefully his capacities and his limitations, and all his choices ought to reflect a continuous and agonizing self-appraisal.

Heightened self-knowledge and the adaptations discussed above require a high price. Personal struggle and suffering are involved. The crucial question is whether a significant number of Americans are able and willing to pay the price. Put another way, the question asks whether Americans can recognize the tasks which this age presents and accept them while accepting also the limitations under which they must act.

We must define the tasks carefully, because the very complexity of our times makes it terribly easy to be caught fighting the wrong battles at the wrong time and in the wrong place. Look at the furor over the question of prayer in the public schools. A dialogue concerning the relation which ought to exist between church and state is valuable and constructive, but those who delude themselves into thinking that an opening prayer makes a secular institution a religious one or that it does something significant by way of protecting historic values are really blind. Instead of strengthening the school in areas where moral problems are involved, such as control or elimination of houseparties and fraternity initiations, or regulation of automobiles by students, or curbing an atheletic program that has become parasitic, these people prefer to fight it out on an oversimplified issue which they can understand and which they hope somehow to control. Then when they do win, which is not very often, they persuade themselves that the devil has been licked. Ironically their success strengthens the very forces they wish to curb.

The real tasks our age presents are numerous and complex. For example, how can we make bureaucracies both efficient and responsible? At the same time how can we enable them to deal more effectively with individual differences? The problem is extraordinarily difficult but not impossible. Some of the most creative thinking going on in educational circles today lends fresh hope to the possibility of making educational institutions more efficient and simultaneously capable of dealing with a wider range of individual differences.

There are many other tasks, but all involve the same attitudes and complexities. Each asks the question of whether we are capable of extending and conserving a heritage which involves self-affirmation and self denial. If we can determine what it is that must be affirmed, we may discover what we must deny in order to make the affirmation. Self-denial has been a consistent theme in our literature and in our experience. Often we hear that the trouble with contemporary Americans is that they are fat; that they have not had to deny themselves anything of consequence. There is an important element of truth in the charge. Is it possible, however, that our failure stems from the fact that we have not related what must be denied to what must be affirmed?

The contemporary age also seems to have marked a central task rather plainly for this generation of Americans. Historically the American people have fought to secure for widening groups of people the circumstances and conditions essential for the achievement of freedom and dignity. One can argue that conditions have often pushed us into the fight. Conditions are pushing us again. The price of preserving the heritage is that of making it applicable in areas we never knew existed. We are today in the position of the nineteenth century men of wealth whose spending was marked by "conspicuous consumption." They learned, with difficulty, that they could not keep their wealth and ignore the "have nots" in their own society. Today Americans find themselves in the middle of a much more vast revolution involving diverse cultures and millions upon millions of people.

The mid-twentieth century American may have some advantages, however. His growing self-awareness may make it possible for him to accept the fact that his efforts will be misunderstood; that he will not get proper credit for what he undertakes. His sense of history may keep him from being easily discouraged and may even allow him to perform his tasks cheerfully. His sense of tragedy will acknowledge the problems on the other side of the mountain. Thus equipped he may discover the applicability to his immediate circumstances of what Paul Tillich has called "the eternal now." That is to say he may discover that in feeding hungry Congolese he is taking a step made necessary by an acceptance of his own past, and made significant for its own sake by the fact that it offers a link with the future.

The problem for the American who has lived at the future rather than in the present is to learn to see life whole; to accept the past which represents his limitations; to enjoy the present for its own sake; and to accept the future with hope, even a future which ends in death. The American heritage, extending back to the days of Puritanism, can be of real service here. Americans in the past have understood that they lived under a judgment which commanded perfection and in circumstances which denied the possibility of achieving it. Born to this agony, the Americans can bear it by accepting the tasks which come out of history and by leading the way toward a future for which they can accept some small, but significant, measure of responsibility.

The miracle of America has been a miracle of rebirth. The miracle has never taken place without pain and suffering; misunderstanding and anguish. But it occurs. We have denied the Negro his rights, but our guilt would not down. We wanted isolation, but we could not make it stick. We dreamed of a nation of farmers, but we surrendered the dream. Put this way the task of those who educate is to initiate a process of self-criticism, to force people to re-examine assumptions, and to look at alien viewpoints. If the educator can help people to discover their limitations, feel sorry about them, and define for themselves responsibilities which are worthy of them, he will have done what he can to help Americans conserve the values that make them what they are.

Curiously enough, the age belongs to the educator in a way. Precisely because this is an age of introspection and analysis, it falls to the intellectual and educator to make the process of maturation significant. If the teacher is content to win smiles and to reinforce complacency, he will kill what Sherwood Anderson called the young thing that keeps us alive. The young thing is, perhaps, man's urge to seek the truth. When men try to possess it, to reduce it to dogma, they kill it. If they do not kill it, however, Americans will have an answer to Nikita Khrushchev's boast that he will bury them. The answer goes something like this. "Our civilization will change, even in ways that we do not foresee. Yours will, too. Your notion of utopia is surely doomed to suffer the fate of all utopias. But you do not understand the source of our strength. The source of our strength is our commitment to seek the truth and to dignify human existence. The source of our strength explains the miracle of our rebirth. For the truth to which we testify is indeed the truth that sets men free. We know that this truth is not our exclusive possession. No one can freeze it, or make it his personal property, but men can witness to the truth and thereby pass on their inheritance to future generations. The thing that gives us strength, the thing to which *we* dedicate *ourselves;* the thing which we affirm and for which we can indeed deny ourselves; that thing *is* eternal."

INDEX

Croevecoeur, Michel de, 85, 104
Cultural Background of Personality, the, 57n.
"cultural lag," 114
Culture, 48-61; defined, 57-58
   & technology, 104-117
Culture and Experience, 61n.
Culture and Social Character: The Work of David Riesman Reviewed, 74n.
"custom," 51, 53; defined, 49

Dade County, 144
Dahl, Robert A., 6, 6n.
Daisy Miller, 87, 90
Darwin, Charles, 144, 159
Degler, Carl N., 153, 153n.
Democracy of the Constitution and Other Essays and Addresses, The, 129n.
Derleth, August, 93
Descartes, Rene, 4
Development of Peirce's Philosophy, The, 48
Dewey, John, 157
Dingwall, Eric John, 78n.
direct constituency representation; theory of 123, 124, 125, 126, 133
Direct Legislation, 125n.
"Disquisition on Government," 124n.
Dodsworth, Sam, 43
Dollard, John, 51, 51n.
"Dominant Profile of American Culture, The," 155n.
Dos Passos, John, 40
Dreams of Reason, The 112n., 113n.
Dreiser, Theodore, 36, 39
DuBois, Cora, 155, 155n.
Dubos, Rene, 112n., 113n.
Duijker, H. C. J., 48n., 57n., 58n.

Edel, Leon, 89n.
Edison, a Biography, 113n.
Edison, Thomas, 113
Edmonds, Walter, 34
Education and World Tragedy, 9n.
Eisenhower, Dwight D., 108
Ekirch, Arthur, 10n.
Elmer Gantry, 33, 42-47, 46n.
Embargo Act, 24
Emerson, Ralph Waldo, 14, 152, 156, 160
Escape from Freedom, 48, 48n.
Ethics of Ambiguity, The, 5n.
Existential Background of Human Dignity, The, 5n.
Existential Psychoanalysis, 5n.
Existentialism, 4, 5, 160

"Fact in Fiction, The," 89n.
Farming; tenant, 141; tree, 142
Farnham, Marynia, 78n.
Farrell, James, 36
Faulkner, William, 36, 37, 38, 162
Federalist, The
   Fed #10, 122

Social Gospel Movement, 108
Social Learning and Imitation, 51n.
Social Process, The, 128n.
Social Science Research Council, 7n.
Social Sciences in Historical Study, The, 7n.
Socialism, 41
"Sociologist as Historian: Riesman's *The Lonely Crowd,* The," 153n.
South, The, 25, 37, 137-50
Southern Baptist Convention, 149
Specialists, 12
Specialization, of work, 71, 72
Spiller, Robert, 10
Sputnik, 162
S-R Theory, see Stimulus-Response Theory
Stages of Economic Growth: a non-Communist Manifesto, The, 111n.
States' rights, 146
Status, concept of, 57
Stimulus-Response Theory, 49-61
Stone, Albert E., Jr., 85
Studies in American Culture: Dominant Ideas and Images, 10, 11n.
Sumner, William Graham, 127, 127n.
Supreme Court, 24, 25, 145-6

Taylor, John, 18
Technology, 103-117, 147, 152
Tennessee Valley Authority, 115
Theatre Arts, 3n.
Theatre in Spite of Itself, The, 3n.
Theatre of the Absurd, 3
Theories of Personality, 48n.
Theology of Culture, 5n.
Theory and Practice in Historical Study, 7n.
Thompson, Kenneth, 6
Thoreau, Henry David, 152, 156, 160
Tillich, Paul, 5n., 165
Titanic, the ship, 156
Tocqueville, Alexis de, 157, 160
Tolstoi, Leo, 33
Tom Sawyer, 86, 88
Toward A General Theory of Action, 58n.
Toynbee, Arnold, 13, 14
Traditionalists, 4, 129
"Tragedy and the New Politics," 162n.
Transcendentalism, 10, 152
"tunnel history," 7n.
Turpie, Mary C., 11n.
Turn of the Screw, The, 85-100
Turner, Fredrick Jackson, 13, 67, 68, 68n., 69, 158
Turner Thesis, 67-68, 69
Twain, Mark, 34, 35n., 39, 86, 88, 160
Two Cultures and the Scientific Revolution, The, 105
"Two Kingdoms of Force: Technology and The Literary Imagination," 107n.
"Typical," defined, 49

Uncle Tom's Cabin, 88
University of South Florida, 144

University of Mississippi, 143-4
University of Texas, 143
Urbanism, 22, 27, 139, 145

"Value," defined, 51
Veblen, Thorstein, 37
Vicary, James M., 80n.
Villon, Francois, 4
Virgin Land, 109n.

Walker, Robert, 8n., 9
War and Peace, 33
War Between the States, see Civil War
War of 1812, 24
Ward, John William, 8, 8n.
Ward, Lester F., 127, 127n.
Washington, George, 16, 37, 53
Webber, George, 163
Webster, Daniel, 25
Weinstein, Arnold, 3
Wells, H. G., 89
Wharton, Edith, 39
What Maisie Knew, 87, 90
Whiting, John W. M., 49-56, 49n., 50n.
Whitman, Walt, 6, 34, 34n., 38, 39
"Whose World? and Welcome to It," 81n.
Williams, Stanley, 10
Willen, Gerald, 90n.
Wilson, Francis G., 119, 119n., 126
Wilson, Woodrow, 156
Winthrop, John, 118
Women, 65-84
Women in the Modern World: Their Education and Their Dilemmas, 79n., 80n.
Women Who Work, 79
Woodward, C. Vann, 9, 9n.
Work, patterns of, for men & women, 72, 73, 140
Wright, Sylvia, 80, 81n.

You Can't Go Home Again, 163
Young, Dr. Francis A., 11

"*Zeitgeist,*" 127, 129
Zoo Story, The, 4